THE ZEN TRADER

Every owner of a physical copy of this edition of

THE ZEN TRADER

can download the eBook for free direct from us at
Harriman House, in a DRM-free format that can be read on any
eReader, tablet or smartphone.

Simply head to:

ebooks.harriman-house.com/zentrader

to get your copy now.

THE ZEN TRADER

*How ancient wisdom can help you
master your mind… and the markets*

Peter Castle

HARRIMAN HOUSE LTD
3 Viceroy Court
Bedford Road
Petersfield
Hampshire
GU32 3LJ
GREAT BRITAIN
Tel: +44 (0)1730 233870

Email: enquiries@harriman-house.com
Website: harriman.house

First published in 2022
Copyright © Peter Castle

Paperback ISBN: 978-0-85719-826-6
eBook ISBN: 978-0-85719-827-3

British Library Cataloguing in Publication Data
A CIP catalogue record for this book can be obtained from the British Library.

I would like to dedicate this book to my parents.

To my mother, Rona Mary Castle, who recognised early in my upbringing that the best role for her as a mother was to trust and let me be the person I wanted to become. And to my father, Kevin Charles Castle, who – despite his conservative and more rigid thinking, coupled with a distrust of the share market – gave me as a Christmas present (in 1999) the book *Market Wizards* and wrote inside the front cover:

> To Pete,
> May you one day too become a Market Wizard!
> Love Dad

CONTENTS

PREFACE

Peter Castle has been a share trader for 27 years, 22 years full time.

Peter Castle (Taishin Shodo) is also an ordained Zen priest.

In this, his second book about trading, Peter explains the wisdom of Zen psychology and its relevance to a trading mindset. To trade well and live happily and successfully, you need calmness and peace of mind; once those qualities of mind are achieved, the understanding of what it means to be truly one with the market will follow.

After many years of studying Buddhism throughout Asia (Vietnam, Thailand, Taiwan and Japan), as well as two years as a monastery resident studying the Tibetan *Kadampa* tradition, Peter was ordained as a priest in the Zen Order of the Boundless Way (*Mugendo Zen Kai*). This tradition is officially recognised and associated with the *Rinzai* Zen tradition of Japan.

FOREWORD

BY DR ALEXANDER ELDER

I have little direct experience with Zen. My closest contact with Buddhism was a decade ago when a townhouse next to mine in midtown Manhattan turned out to be a small Buddhist monastery. I went to a few of their public events. The chief guy, an American, had a car, a girlfriend, owned a farm in a neighboring state, and enjoyed his steak and wine. Very pleasant people, albeit quite far from the Western canon of poverty, chastity, and obedience.

In reading Peter's manuscript, I immediately saw his focus on trading psychology – the essential factor in any trader's success or failure. The crucial role of psychology is something that many traders and most beginners don't recognize.

The technical side of trading is quite straightforward. Analyzing markets, we deal with only five numbers for any bar or a candle: open, high, low, and closing prices, along with volume. A handful of technical indicators will help you analyze those numbers and reach a reasonable conclusion whether there is a trade in the first place, and if there is, should it be from the long or the short side. This is something I can teach an average person in less than a week.

Developing sound trading psychology takes a lot longer. It could be years. There are several paths you can take to develop the necessary attitudes and skills. You need to select a path that emotionally appeals to you and stay on it. Peter's Zen is one of those options.

In my first book I wrote how to apply the principles of Alcoholics Anonymous to trading, particularly loss avoidance. In recent years I began to stress the importance of record-keeping in order to learn from your experiences. I say: "Show me a trader with good records, and I'll show you a good trader."

At a conference in Texas, I met an old lady, a former school librarian, who became an active and highly successful trader after retiring and receiving an inheritance. She was very religious and considered herself a steward of the Lord's money. She'd pray and trade, and if a trade went even slightly against her, she exited quickly because the money "wasn't hers to lose."

The point here is that every successful trader has their psychology tightly organized. Each of us needs to find our path to success. By picking Peter's book you're making an important step in the right direction. As you read his engaging and personal book, you'll soon discover whether his Zen approach appeals to you.

I wish you success,

Dr Alexander Elder
SpikeTrade.com
New York, 2021

INTRODUCTION

THIS book is written with a purpose: to compare and connect the methods of trading to the philosophies and techniques of Zen. The intention is to show the reader that embracing Zen in their trading and life will improve not only their financial situation, but also their happiness and overall well-being.

Each chapter shows comparisons between trading and Zen, and demonstrates how adopting a Zen approach will elevate your performance as a trader (or investor) and bring more peace and profit into your life.

Many professional traders talk about their *edge*. For example, an edge can be a trading system based on mathematical probability. Another trading edge may be taking advantage of market anomalies, or perhaps trading non-correlated markets to spread risk and reduce portfolio volatility. Those are just three examples of many. However, this book offers you the greatest edge of all: a Zen mindset.

A major goal in my trading career has been to make money as safely and easily as possible, without complex, time-consuming methods.

Another equally important goal was to be able to trade with minimal stress.

So how have I, as a full-time trader for 20 years, managed to do that? To survive, profit and keep my sanity? Well, I haven't; and then on the other hand, I have. If that sounds paradoxical, perhaps it is. Zen can be like that.

Let me explain.

One of my first trading teachers claimed that many are attracted to trading for the wrong reasons. My assumption was that I was not one of those people. However, the realisation occurred (unfortunately, much later than I would have preferred) that I too was in that category. As aspiring traders, we think we know ourselves well, but many of us do not.

The same teacher warned me that the market would target me like a heat-seeking missile, and find any emotional frailties or weaknesses I had. That was a challenging opinion. On the one hand, I didn't believe it; but on the other, there lay an uncomfortable feeling. Now, with hindsight, I am aware it was one of my first experiences in realising I didn't really know myself that well, and I certainly wasn't listening to my intuition.

When I started trading in 1995, I was fit, well read, well travelled, confident, successful in my business and the owner of some property investments. However, even at my relatively young age, I knew myself well enough to realise that the challenge of trading would not be financial, technical or academic – but emotional. An honest admission is I had no idea what I was letting myself in for.

Full-time trading was tough. I started in January 2000: it was a baptism by fire. In March 2000, US tech stocks crashed, driving down markets all over the globe. The 9/11 terrorist attacks came in 2001 and markets again went down, not recovering until, in 2003, the first bomb was dropped on Baghdad, starting the Iraq War.

It was one of my first important lessons in how markets hate uncertainty. Once the US-led coalition decided to invade Iraq, removing a large element of political uncertainty, markets went up. From then on, markets continued rising until the sub-prime rumours started in 2007, culminating in the Global Financial Crisis (GFC) crash in 2008. I missed the early market move up from 2003 to 2005 but managed to catch a big part of the rally between 2006 and 2007.

Over the ups and downs, I managed to generate profits here and there, and survived. But I remember often thinking, "Wow, someone could make a *lot* of money from trading if they knew what they were doing."

It was around this time I started looking at why I wouldn't or couldn't stick to my systems. Some bad habits had crept into my trading. I was a good analyst and, being a visual and creative person, I could remember things like chart patterns, a stock's volatility or price behaviour, and how a lot of trends seem to start in the same way. However, I couldn't stick to any ideas. I kept changing my mind, looking for different techniques and methods. I was easily distracted away from one method I had developed only to revisit it later and discover how well it had performed. Analysis wasn't the problem; I had a good win rate with my decision making. At one point, despite a 90% win rate when trading an options campaign for several months, I failed to make any money due solely to my atrocious lack of discipline in committing to sell orders. Poor and inconsistent trade-sizing methods didn't help either. The problem was something deeper, and I was determined to find it.

I came across an unlikely signpost on my trading journey: Alcoholics Anonymous.

Early in 2003, I had taken myself off to a country town to renovate a small cottage. I was tired, frustrated, depressed and in desperate need of a break from trading. As I painted the house, I listened to the local radio station, where I kept hearing ads for AA meetings. Remembering the trading coach Dr Elder's recommendation to attend an AA meeting, I did so (even though I was confident I was not an alcoholic). My brief association with AA was my first truly spiritual experience, for what I learned was that the AA's 12-step programme is a spiritual method of rehabilitation. The lesson Dr Elder was attempting to teach me became clear. I had some issues I needed to work on – the main one being my addiction to the market and trading.

An alcoholic I wasn't, but a gambler I was.

I started to notice something peculiar about trading coaches and others I was reading about. Dr Elder was a fan of AA and its spiritual message. Ed Seykota, well known for his trend-following methodologies, devoted many pages of his website to his own brand of spirituality, a blend of Buddhist and American Indian philosophies. Mark Douglas's work was rooted in Eastern philosophy and modern psychology, expressed in his book *Trading in the Zone* (Penguin, 2000). Dr Van Tharp was a practitioner and devotee of Oneness Organisation from Chennai, India – an organisation steeped in the spiritual traditions of Hinduism. In Australia, the trading and investing coach Colin Nicholson (although with no direct spiritual affiliation) often talked about the need for gratefulness, emotional intelligence and delayed gratification – all spiritual concepts from the sages of old.

Then, of course, there is me and my interest in Zen. So, what is it that makes Zen different to these other forms of thinking – particularly as a way of thinking most suited to trading?

In my opinion, there are two obstacles to trading success. Zen can solve both of them.

In my first book, *Mindful Trading using Winning Probability*, I explained that those obstacles are:

1. Traders don't have a system or method to trade.

2. Even if they do have a method, they don't stick to it.

My first book was devoted to the first issue and a very simple trend-following method was explained in detail. This new book explains and breaks down the second obstacle that affects almost every trader and is a major barrier to success in the markets. During that process, we delve into Zen and explore why it is such a powerful tool to have in your trading toolbox.

If we are to use Zen as a trading tool, how does one reconcile the philosophy of Zen Buddhism with trading, as at first glance they might appear to be in direct conflict with each other?

My initial motives for getting into trading were chiefly self-interested. I had goals I wanted to achieve – and to accomplish those goals I needed money. However, apart from money, one of the most important goals was an alternative lifestyle to the one I was living. Becoming tired of the daily grind of being the owner/manager of a busy car repair business prompted the desire to create better balance in my life. From the beginning of my trading career, I was well aware that continuing self-development would be a large component of the challenge before me. Spirituality, Buddhism and finally Zen came about from my interest and desire to develop as a person. My life's journey – from leaving a private boarding school at age 16 to start a trade as a car spray painter, then becoming a small businessman/share trader/teacher and now an ordained Zen priest – has surprised me perhaps more than anyone else.

One of the many similarities between trading and Zen is that when you learn something, you think you know it. Upon revisiting the lesson perhaps years later, you see the whole thing in a different light. Before publishing this book, I gave it to some of my more experienced clients to read. I received a common response: they would not have appreciated or understood the content as a beginner trader as much as they do now. So, if you are a beginner, when you finish reading this book, come back later and re-read it. If you are an intermediate or experienced trader, you will be nodding your head in agreement and also be awakened to new possibilities and knowledge.

Attaining a calm and peaceful mind is often mentioned in this book. In this hectic and sometimes crazy world in which we live, those qualities can be rare. As I write, the world is in the midst of the Covid crisis – a perfect example of how unpredictable and uncertain life can quickly become. From trading full time for two decades, along with teaching trading for more than ten years, it is my experience that calmness and a peaceful mind are the missing ingredients for most traders. In fact, as a Zen practitioner, I find these same ingredients are missing for some of those on the Zen path. It can be a simple path, but because of our human complexities we make both trading and Zen difficult. Somehow, we need to make things simpler.

We humans bring our strengths and weaknesses to every circumstance of life. As we say in Zen, "You take your mind with you wherever you go." Until you can be calm in the chaos around you and have the presence of mind to act accordingly, peace and profit will be elusive.

We live in a world of incredible knowledge and resources. There are thousands of books, courses, coaches, computer programmes and webinars about trading; the list is almost endless. There is no shortage of technical know-how.

There are also thousands of books and courses on mindset and meditation. Psychologists and psychiatrists have devised methods and self-development courses in trading. Medications, supplements and even stimulants are available to assist the aspiring trader.

Despite all of the above, the success rate of traders is still low.

Is it all too hard? Is it even possible? Or is it that we are all looking in the wrong place?

I believe it is the latter. This book will address that situation by using Zen: a mindset and way of life renowned for its clarity and calm. If being successful is about modelling successful methods or people, then modelling a method that creates peace and calm is what is needed to be a good trader. We all started trading to bring more opportunity and freedom into our lives – not more suffering.

The similarities between trading and Zen are immense. Both are simple processes but not necessarily easy to follow. However, the rewards are also immense – both personally and professionally. As traders and also as humans wanting to evolve and improve who we are, we need to look at methods that work. Methods that have merit and are proven over time. Zen is such a method.

1

THE TWO OBSTACLES TO YOUR TRADING SUCCESS

I *N* my opinion trading is easy, but we make it difficult. We make it difficult because we experience two obstacles to success. I mentioned these in the introduction, but they are worth repeating:

1. Traders don't have a system or method to trade.

2. Even if they do have a method, they don't stick to it.

IDENTIFYING AND IMPLEMENTING A TRADING METHOD

As mentioned in the introduction, many trading methods are about probability, often using systems with set rules to produce a mathematical edge. A mathematical edge does not need to be complex. An edge is simply when the probability of your method can consistently deliver more profits than losses. A mathematical trading edge can be obtained in many ways, and there are many different methods that provide an edge. However, for most traders a numerical edge is not enough to overcome the problem of not sticking to a method – because of their intense emotions.

My first book, *Mindful Trading using Winning Probability*, focuses on method and probability, showing you why and where the edges are in a robust trading system. That system has a win rate of around 50% and a winner-to-loser ratio of nearly 4 to 1. I will discuss a similar system later in this book. (I suggest you don't go looking for it now. If you do, you will be committing a typical error of losing traders – impatience!) Since the winning trades make almost four times the losing trades, it should be obvious to you that if you stick to it, over time the system will be highly profitable.

Many traders do not have a system based on probability; they begin trading without a sound method. Preferably, they should employ a method that is as simple as possible, which makes it easy for aspiring traders to take the first steps along the path to trading mastery. Most aspiring traders are not taught a simple method at the beginning of their education. They often attempt too many methods or are taught complex and confusing methods, making processes hard to adhere to.

An example of a simple training process can be found in the movie *The Karate Kid*. The Japanese martial arts master teaches his student to polish cars by *waxing on* with one hand and *waxing off* with the other – a seemingly unimportant and boring process. It is only later, while defending himself during a competition fight, that the student realises the significance of mastering the basics of repetitive and co-ordinated hand movements.

I know from my own trading experience, and from observing colleagues and students, that many traders will struggle to trust and implement not only my systems but any system or method – even one they have developed themselves, no matter how simple it may be.

THE DIFFICULTY OF STICKING TO A METHOD

Not being able to stick to a method is something many traders don't realise is a problem. It seems to take beginners a few years to come to the realisation that they are self-sabotaging their performance. No matter how logical, rational, convincing or seemingly robust a trading system is; no matter whether it is operated manually, automatically or under the advice of another; the overall success of the strategy is determined by the trader's ability to cope with their emotions, which are created by their interpretation of market volatility.

There are as many methods as there are traders, and as mentioned, the percentage of successful traders is very low: as low as 5% to 10%. Obviously, there is another obstacle to trading success apart from just sourcing a simple trading method with a mathematical edge.

The reason why you (or other traders) won't stick to a method is not complicated: the simple answer is *fear*. Fear of an undesirable outcome, coupled with complicated and often confusing emotions that arise when traders are faced with uncertainty.

Many trading experts have offered opinions about the psychology involved in trading. Below I list some of the prevalent advice and opinions – many I am sure you have discovered yourself or heard about before:

- Deeply accepting losses is the holy grail of trading.
- You need to be peaceful and calm – but strike quickly when needed.
- The only guarantee in trading is that you will lose.
- The most important skill is accepting losses.
- It is not about the perfect method, but the perfect mind.
- Do not repeat the same non-working process.

- Your rules are only as strong as the emotions that created those rules.

- Your subconscious rules your behaviour.

- Trading is all about your subconscious programming.

- The subconscious determines how much money you win or lose.

- Even smart people lose, because of their emotions and subconscious.

- When a trade goes against you, you get nervous and uptight. You can't think straight.

- The market works by taking money from emotional traders and giving it to calm traders.

- Master traders lose often.

- Master traders do not take losses personally.

- Master traders separate their ego and identity from their trading performance.

- Master traders don't care about losing.

- Master traders don't have the need for instant gratification.

- Master traders have no need for external gratification about their identity.

- Trading is gambling.

- You are embarrassed when you lose.

- Losing makes you feel less of a man (or woman, but the majority of traders are men).

- Trading will give you instant feedback about being a failure.

- Your mind destroys your trading results.

- You feel you are not good enough.

- If you feel like a loser, the next trade you take will generate a loss.

- Don't beat yourself up about losing, just accept it.

- Your trading challenges reflect the flaws in your personality.

- You need massive guts to be a good trader.

If this list continued, it would fill the chapter – but I am sure you get the idea about the complexity of emotions that arise when we trade. So, it is understandable that even after years of study and perhaps expensive training to learn how to trade, many traders cannot trade successfully. Clearly, something is wrong with what is being taught about how traders can cope. Not just cope, but succeed – and finally deal with the demons that plague their trading results.

Therefore, we need to explore why traders find it so difficult to commit to their chosen method, whether that method is systematic or discretionary. If it really is just fear that creates the bulk of trading challenges, how can Zen remove that obstacle?

A problem can have a simple solution, yet we seem to want a complicated answer. In Zen, many answers to problems are simple. I am going to show you why Zen is the solution – a simple solution. Mastering the techniques may not be easy, but I assure you it is the answer that will prevent fear from hindering your success.

A ZEN SAYING

If you can solve the problem
Then what is the need of worrying?
If you cannot solve it
Then what is the use of worrying?

———

CHAPTER SUMMARY

- Trading itself can be simple, but the emotions of trading are often difficult.

- Most traders find it difficult to commit to a method – even one that has a good probability of winning.

- There is a solution that empowers us to overcome the fear of trading.

2

ZEN IS THE SOLUTION TO THE SECOND OBSTACLE

THE term *obstacle* (the word *hindrance* is also often used) in Zen refers to a roadblock in your mind. Such obstacles are like having something in the way of your path, preventing you from going the way you want to. However, in this case I am talking more about a mental obstacle than a physical one. The Buddha had a lot to say about these invisible boundaries in our minds.

AN INTRODUCTION TO ZEN

Before continuing, I want to emphasise what a challenging task it is to explain Zen – for Zen is more an experience (like trading) than a theory to be described. There are many others before me, far more learned than I, who have attempted to explain what some regard as the unexplainable. Despite that, here is my humble attempt to explain the similarities between the great and challenging profession of trading and the profound philosophies of Zen. To get the full experience of Zen, you need to *do* it rather than read about it – just one of the many correlations between trading and Zen. I regard trading as a *trade* and any trade you wish to master requires theory *and* practice: you won't become a master trader without taking risks and *actually* trading.

Likewise, you won't gain great awareness in Zen without doing the practice. Theory alone is not enough.

Zen has no religious expectations and does not ask you to believe in anything. In fact, it encourages doubt and free thinking – the exact qualities you also need in order to become a good trader. Zen is perhaps more aligned with the Great Spirit concept of the Native Americans, or the Taoist philosophy of being in flow with nature and accepting the harshness and beauty of life, or what some call *what is*.

It's important to make a few things clear about Zen Buddhism. Zen is more a philosophy and life system than a religion. Religion is defined by the *Oxford English Dictionary* as, "The belief in and worship of a superhuman controlling power, especially a personal God or gods." This is not Zen.

It may help us to understand the simple philosophy of Zen if we consider some Buddhist history.

Zen Buddhism respects the teachings of the Buddha, but he is not regarded as a superhuman controlling power or a god. The Buddha was human, an academic and a member of royalty. He belonged to the Shakya class, renowned for their warrior and ministerial skills as well as their scientific and artistic abilities.

The Buddha became frustrated with the religions of his day and the many varied belief systems, so he made a sweeping statement. In fact, he made four, and he called them the Four Noble Truths, which are:

1. Life is suffering (the word *suffering* has often been interpreted as *discontent*).

2. The cause of suffering (discontent) is attachment.

3. It is possible to end suffering.

4. There is a method to achieve the end of suffering.

The four statements above can be narrowed down to two that are most relevant to traders: life is suffering, and the cause of suffering is attachment. That is, trading produces a lot of discontent, and we produce the suffering ourselves because of our attachment to the outcome of our trades.

Or described another way: no one likes to lose or feel like a failure; it deeply affects our mental equilibrium.

LEAPS IN REALISATION

The realisation that the first obstacle to trading success is not having a probable method is a quantum leap in your development as a trader. I consider using a probable method to be the beginning of trading mastery. However, the biggest killers of trading success are stress and worry. Unfortunately, even a good method does not seem to solve that issue for most traders. Many of us entered the markets with the intention of improving our lives through financial independence, not to make life more challenging than it already can be. Stress and worry are brought about through uncertainty, and for some traders fear is compounded by the trauma of past losses.

Trauma triggered by financial loss is not an easy thing to recover from. Some people never recover and carry a fear of trading or investing for the rest of their lives. For some experienced traders, the trauma of trading exists for many years as a state of frustration – a frustration brought about from continually low or negative results. However, if you can eliminate stress and replace troubling emotions with a calm and peaceful mind (as a result of detaching), you will be able to trade better. Much better.

Accepting *what is*, learning non-attachment, recognising and releasing trauma, and opening their minds to new philosophies and ways of thinking are not what traders initially think they need to do. Although most traders eventually attain the realisation that the emotional challenges of trading are inhibiting their performance, they do not yet realise it is the obstacle of attachment that is the real roadblock. They start looking for other solutions to the problem and avoiding the work of personal introspection, often falling into the trap of attempting to over-control their trading accounts by using ever more complex strategies. This rarely works.

Pete's personal trading story

I WAS IN Japan attending a retreat as part of my preparation for ordination. Although this trip had nothing to do with trading education, I never miss the chance to recognise and examine the similarities between trading and Zen. Every evening after dinner, the abbot and I would walk, normally in silence. Zen masters are renowned for their use of few words and their sometimes annoyingly brief and seemingly obscure answers. At our halfway point, a lookout over the Sea of Japan, I turned to him and asked, "If there was one piece of advice – only one – that you would give to an aspiring practitioner, what would it be?"

Without hesitation, and in perfect English, his heavy accent mysteriously disappearing in that moment, he turned to me and said, "Personal introspection," followed by a heavily accented, "Now let's walk back." We walked back in silence; my lesson was over for that day.

A ZEN SAYING

Obstacles
do not block the path;
they are the path.

CHAPTER SUMMARY

- Zen is a philosophy and way of life, rather than a religion.

- Trading and life are tough; the key to winning and to stop suffering is to learn non-attachment.

- Personal introspection is an important factor in being successful.

3

OBSTACLES
OF LOGIC

RATHER than learning to detach, traders seek maximum control in an attempt to deal with the second obstacle. They apply the following form of logic and combine that logic with maximum control. For example, the following thinking among traders is common and it seems logical, but it is not using the powerful method of Zen detachment.

Traders think if they trade frequently and successfully, a huge amount of money can be made. However, within those two words – *frequently* and *successfully* – lies the challenge.

Many traders think that the more they shorten their trading time frame, the better. However, *better* also requires that their methods realise a higher rate of success. That is because in many cases, a shorter trading time frame can dramatically tilt the mathematical probability of consistently winning with a big payoff ratio to the downside. For many traders, it is within the longer-term trends of daily, weekly and even monthly time frames that large amounts of money can be made. I am sure many of you have short-term traded stocks for what you thought was a good profit, only to re-examine the stock later to see that it has rocketed well beyond your exit price. Often with trading, fewer trades can mean more profit. Exerting less control and flowing with the movements of the market often results in a better outcome, and that methodology can apply to any trading time frame.

TIME IS A DIFFICULT CHOICE

Directly linked to the matter of control, one of the hardest decisions you will need to make when trading is: what trading time frame will you use to execute your method? Most beginners start with analysing and then trading stock prices in a daily time frame. Focusing the majority of their attention on analysing daily charts creates an expectation – and then a need – to analyse charts and individual stock performance intra-day. The analysis of charts over intra-day time scales then seems to lead to a desire to shorten the time frame to four-hourly or even less, perhaps hourly or even ten- or five-minute charts. The problem here is you are not focusing on what is most important: developing your mind to detach from undesirable outcomes.

In fact, you are doing the opposite: attempting to exert more control over an uncontrollable situation. You cannot control the market by viewing it in a shorter time frame, but you can control how you respond to it. Notice I did not use the word *react*, for it is the heedless reactions in your trading that Zen will help eliminate.

Some traders shorten their trading time frame because they think this is the requirement to make a lot of money. What they are not aware of is the strong possibility they are simply reacting to unpleasant feelings – feelings created by their thoughts about the market movements. Unpleasant feelings create a desire to control. The control they have at their fingertips is to buy and sell frequently – to alleviate uncomfortable emotions. But now they are likely just compounding existing obstacles, and creating new ones.

FREQUENT TRADING CAN INCREASE OBSTACLES

Considering that statistically 90% to 95% of traders lose or break even, one of the reasons for poor performance is probably that they are buying and selling at the wrong time. This can be a result of trading too often.

Increasing your time frame to weekly, or even monthly, charts for analysis and even trading could be the best option to put you in an area where the winners exist. Away from the anxiety-ridden losers poring over charts every day.

My personal trading experience and coaching of others leave me in no doubt that shorter-term trading is more challenging than longer-term trading. However, many find longer-term trading difficult, because of the challenges of boredom and the need to practise delayed gratification. It seems as if there is no escaping the emotional component of trading, whether you trade short term or long term. Whatever your time scale preference or goals, stepping back for a look at the big picture can assist you in detaching from the short-term movements of the market. After all, detachment is key.

FREQUENT TRADING AND MENTAL HEALTH

My trading partner once described frequent trading as "being sucked into the market vortex." As any experienced trader will tell you, that vortex can be very stressful, particularly when trading in short time frames. So, a re-examination of your trading time frame can improve both trading results and your mental health.

However, regardless of what time frame you use to trade, the market movements will challenge you, sometimes to what can feel like – or can in fact be – breaking point.

It seems whatever strategy or time frame a trader uses has its challenges. The obstacle that is the root cause of poor performance in trading is the inability of the trader to detach. Attempting to control the market by complicated or short-term systems is not a long-term solution. The solution is to learn the Zen skill of detachment – a technique that will be discussed at length in the following chapters. To satisfy the reader with an appetite for more risk or trade frequency, we will look at some shorter-term trading methods later. However, in the meantime, consider the results achieved from the weekly trend trading system below: a system averaging just one trade a week. A result like this can only be achieved by using a method with winning probability, then being able to detach from the inevitable adverse movements any system produces.

Pete's personal trading story

HERE IS AN example of how detaching from the daily movements of the market can be very profitable. In 2005 a trading friend showed me a weekly trend trading system. It had just three rules: buy a stock's 52-week closing high; give preference to the lowest-priced stock; then use a trailing stop as your exit (average true range of three calculated over four weeks). Figure 3.1 is a simulation chart of the result on the Australian ASX 300 using accurate adjusted data. The method averages only 38 trades a year and risks just 1.5% of total portfolio equity per trade. This leads to an end result of A$6 million from starting capital of A$100,000. At the time I thought it was interesting, but was convinced I could do much better trading on a daily time frame. I started using the system but became impatient and never stuck with it, thinking that short-term methods would be more rewarding. The Zen saying that follows sums up the value of a good idea, combined with commitment and time.

Figure 3.1: Australian ASX 300 (simulation)

Source: wealth-lab.com

A ZEN SAYING

An idea that is developed and put into action is more important than an idea that exists only as an idea.

—

CHAPTER SUMMARY

- Many traders are impatient, think control is the answer and want instant gratification.
  - Less (trading) can be more (money).

THE BUDDHA HAD
A SYSTEM

AS mentioned in the previous chapter, the Buddha wrote the Four Noble Truths:

1. Life is suffering.

2. The cause of suffering is attachment.

3. The ending of suffering is possible.

4. There is a method (system) to achieve the end of suffering.

For traders, the first two are most important. Here they are again with a change of phrasing.

1. Trading and life can be tough.

2. To make trading and life easier, we need to learn detachment.

I have come to the same conclusion about trading that the Buddha did about life. If trading and life are difficult and the cause is attachment, a method to master non-attachment is the answer.

THE BUDDHA'S INITIAL SYSTEM

After the Buddha taught the Four Noble Truths, guess what happened next? People wanted more.[1] People – particularly traders – always want more. However, without method and non-attachment, *more* can turn into madness.

The Buddha's initial method of teaching was perhaps a little naïve. To paraphrase him slightly, he said "Go sit on your backside, meditate and find for yourself who you truly are; then see if you agree with my ideas." One of the great appeals of Buddhism is the encouragement of doubt, free thinking, asking questions and not relying on a set of dogmatic rules or an external superpower for the answers. You are encouraged to find the answers and strength within, not from outside of you; very different to my dogmatic religious upbringing and many other belief systems. Zen is often called *the faith of no faith* – perfect for agnostic or atheist traders or for those happy with their existing religion or belief system.

However, like many traders who want to burrow down into extreme technical detail, followers of the Buddha were the same. They asked, "Should we eat meat? What can we drink? What about sex? How much do we meditate? How do we live and work? How should we think and behave?" And so on…

Traders ask, "Will the markets rise or fall? Is it a good time to buy? What do I do? What would you do? Which is the best technical indicator?" And so on…

---

[1] Thich Nhat Hanh, *Old Path White Clouds* (Penguin Books, 2016).

THE SYSTEM THE BUDDHA DEVELOPED AND ZEN

So, to satisfy people's need to know what to do, the Buddha and his closest followers became system developers. They developed rules and regulations – dos and don'ts. The result? Buddhism went the way good ideas often do, getting caught up in the details while attempting to provide people with all the answers. The initial advice – "Go sit on your backside and meditate," to explore your doubts and truly know yourself – was mostly disregarded.

Until Zen came along.

Buddhism originated in India and spread south to Sri Lanka and east to China (where it blended with Taoism and became *Chan*). It then moved to Southeast Asian countries like Vietnam and Thailand, and then northeast again to Japan, where the word *Chan* became *Zen*.

A Japanese monk called Dogen (1200–1253) was the man responsible for the change and development of Zen in Japan. Dissatisfied with the way Buddhism had become hierarchical, at times overly religious and superstitious, Dogen encouraged students to follow the Buddha's original advice, which was – you guessed it – "Go sit on your backside, meditate and find for yourself who you truly are; then see if you agree with my ideas." No one can, or should, tell you what to do or how to live your life, because it is your choice and responsibility. You can be guided, but ultimately it's your call.

Doesn't this sound like trading?

Buddhism takes on its own flavour in whatever country it exists in, influenced by the prevailing culture. Tibetan Buddhism is quite religious, similar in some ways to Catholicism and many other Christian belief systems. Chinese Buddhism is superstitious. Some of the Southeast Asian traditions are very austere. Japan's Zen is strict and pragmatic. In Western countries – particularly the USA, Australia, the

UK, and Canada – mindfulness has been the main export of Buddhism. In my opinion, mindfulness is more an advertising buzzword than the key to peace of mind and trading mastery. If I want to attract a crowd of people to teach meditation, I use the word *mindfulness*. If I use the words *focus, discipline, regular meditation, behavioural consistency, moral values* (not popular in the West), I know I won't get a crowd at all; it's therefore better to use the word *mindfulness* to attract interest. The strategy of advertising mindfulness is used by Buddhist centres, corporations, health food shops and hippy-trippy meditation teachers all throughout Western culture.

MINDFULNESS ALONE IS NOT THE SYSTEM

It is worth mentioning early in this book that **mindfulness alone is not detachment.**

Mindfulness was just one of the requirements of training that the Buddha encouraged. Mindfulness on its own, although important, won't make you a master trader. Zen is a perfect fit for trading because it teaches discipline, focus, acceptance and (you might not like to hear this) moral values. Is the teaching of moral values in Zen a religious hang-up? Absolutely not. Its purpose is to protect your mind, and your peace of mind. Ask any trader who has tried to be successful while having an affair or indulging in drugs, sex, gambling, food, alcohol or even an exercise addiction: they will verify that these pastimes are unhealthy coping strategies, often a result of a stressed and turbulent state of mind.

Addictions and unhealthy coping strategies attempt to relieve stress, but are also avoidance strategies offering escape from the emotional challenges of change, particularly changing the way you respond to your thoughts.

To be a successful trader, you can't keep avoiding who you truly are and asking yourself why you make the choices you do. This is why the Buddha said, "Go sit on your backside, meditate and find for yourself who you truly are; then see if you agree with my ideas."

Good trading is often boring. Avoiding your personal problems by trading (especially if you are just gambling for excitement or avoidance) will kill your profits. It might even kill you. To be a consistently successful trader over the long term, you will need to face your demons, not run away from them. Turning to face your demons is like being assertive to a bully at school or work. If you do that, they often back down. Being aggressive is just the bully's coping strategy; when you realise this, you will also realise they are ultimately weaker than you. Zen will give you the insight and strength to cope with the market bully; the one that makes you scared, that exposes you to all manner of intense negative emotions. You will develop insight and strength by following the Buddha's system.

Pete's personal trading story

I FIRST STARTED trading in 1995, while working very hard in my car repair business. The business was successful, but I was unhappy, restless and wanting out. I was also in a long-term romantic relationship with which I was unhappy, restless and wanting out. I saw trading as my escape route from both. I became addicted to trading as an aversion to what was really required: confronting my work and personal problems. My trading was emotional, irrational, totally unstructured and extremely stressful. Through good luck, perhaps some skill and the raging tech market of the late 1990s I managed to make a little money. I traded like this for three years until I decided I needed to either give up trading or devote myself more to the profession. In early 2000 I took the plunge, sold my business and became a full-time trader. However, my personal problems remained. In fact, they amplified with the stress of no regular income, the dotcom crash of 2000 and then the attack on the

New York Twin Towers in 2001. As I said earlier, it was a baptism by fire: my personal life, physical health and mental well-being suffered greatly – not to mention my trading account! The root cause of my unhappiness and lack of success was avoidance. Avoiding the hard work in making the tough calls and cleaning up my act.

I took a break from trading to help a mate renovate a house he owned in a small country town in southern New South Wales. I also bought a house in the same town for $80,000 and sold it a year later for $150,000. With a clearer mind and my confidence back, I resumed trading; but as the Buddha said, life is suffering – and for me there was more suffering to come, because I had not yet mastered the correct way of thinking.

A ZEN SAYING

The mind is everything – what you think, you become.

CHAPTER SUMMARY

- You should doubt everything, including trading systems and Zen.

- You need to get to know who you are.

- Being mindful alone, although important, won't make you a master trader.

- Awareness and not indulging in avoidance are the beginnings of the path to becoming a master trader.

- There is a system of thinking that will make you a master trader.

CORRECT UNDERSTANDING OF ATTACHMENT PRODUCES CLARITY OF THOUGHT

*I*f letting go of attachment is the solution to obstacles, let me explain what that actually means.

The philosophy of non-attachment in Zen Buddhism is not well understood. If it is the cause of all our problems in trading and life, what exactly was the Buddha talking about? Some psychologists have the opinion that Zen attachment philosophy is a complicated avoidance strategy to help one cope with life. My opinion is that, like most traders, many mental health professionals are misinformed or do not understand the Zen meaning of *attachment*. In some cases, perhaps these doubting psychologists make a fair point: there are some Buddhist practitioners who do not understand attachment and use non-attachment as an avoidance of responsibility, confusing themselves and others – particularly loved ones.

For many, the term *attachment* brings to mind those of a personal nature – love for a spouse, child, relative, pet, friend etc. More accurately, Zen is asking you to detach from *emotion*. This request can be a stumbling block for those who mistakenly see it as a robotic or even cold approach to life.

Zen's requirement to detach from someone is *not* a request to stop loving. It is a request to stop obsessing, worrying, controlling or participating in any other negative emotion about your relationship with a person or thing. The philosophy is similar in a way to one you have perhaps heard before: "Set it free, and if it is truly yours, it will return." Similar, except that *it* was never yours to own and control in the first place.

An example of unhealthy attachment would be a jealous spouse or partner: one who constantly checks on, questions or accuses the other of inappropriate behaviour. As an example, let us presume the accused party is innocent, therefore the behaviour from the accuser is one of obsession, worry or control – not of love. Obsessing, worrying and wanting to control are emotions and actions displayed by people who are insecure. They are often frightened of an outcome they do not desire, such as being betrayed or left for another, and therefore experiencing loss. In this case, the controlling person's attachment to a possible loss becomes the obstacle to their mental clarity – they are unable to clearly distinguish between facts and emotions.

Another example of attachment may be to physical objects, such as one's house or car. As mentioned earlier, I owned a car repair business before I became a full-time trader. It was not uncommon for customers to be more concerned about the damage to their car than about the damage (physical or psychological) to a fellow passenger. The customers' mental attachment to the object, in this case the car, took precedence over their thinking about the well-being of another human. Often, they would be so distressed at the loss or damage to their physical object that they would be incapable of conversing with any clarity or completing simple paperwork. It was not until I reminded them that they and others were healthy and unhurt that they were able to reprioritise their thinking and became more calm, rational and functional.

An extreme example of unhealthy attachment is debilitating grief – the intense emotion that can be experienced following the death of a loved one. The griever's attachment to loving that person holds them in an eternal state of grief, making their life miserable. In this case,

Zen is not asking the suffering person to let go of the love for the deceased, but to let go of their *attachment* to the love of the one they have lost. Holding on to a loss, in this case the extreme loss of a loved one, perpetuates suffering and blocks the possibility of experiencing a winning situation – such as, perhaps, new love. New love may not be another person but rather other experiences or situations life has to offer. Staying attached to what was (the person being alive) prevents the mind from opening to new possibilities. Grief is a normal human experience. However, in this situation, *attachment to the emotion of grief (not the experience of grief itself)* is the mind's obstacle to new beginnings and happiness.

The consequences of unchecked attachment are far-reaching, impacting not only personal but also societal and cultural relationships. Arguably, the most destructive and senseless attachment of all is an ideology that results in war. Serious conflict can eventuate because of the attachment to a belief (or set of beliefs) that one culture's way of life and ideas are superior to another culture's way of life and ideas. These beliefs can be so strong that some people think they have the right to kill another – at times millions of others – to impose their group's opinions and ideology. This is one reason why some people detest religions. History can certainly give that opinion merit. There is no doubt history shows us that attachment to dogmatic and inflexible beliefs becomes the obstacle to reconciliation, compromise and peace.

ATTACHMENT AND STRONG EMOTIONS IN TRADING

To exemplify how attachment and losses apply to trading, consider what traders experience during epic events such as the GFC in 2008 or – more recently – the Covid crash of 2020. I have had students so attached to their negative experience of the GFC that they stayed out of the market for the following ten years. They were so attached to the loss that they couldn't let go of that experience, blocking them from the possibility of experiencing a winning situation. In this example, attachment to losses of the past – be that the GFC or other trading experiences – becomes the obstacle in the trader's mind. It prevents them from thinking calmly and rationally about the markets as they are now, rather than how they were then.

An interesting side note here is the experience of Edwin Coppock, inventor of the Coppock Curve indicator. Edwin had been asked by the Episcopal Church of the USA to identify buying opportunities for long-term investors. He considered that market downturns were like bereavements, which required a period of mourning from loss. With this comparison in mind, he asked the church bishops how long it normally took for people to recover from grief. Their answer was 11 to 14 months. He then used those periods in his calculations. It is interesting to note that when the market downtrend started at the beginning of the GFC in 2008, it bottomed 14 months later (late February 2009), before starting an uptrend in March 2009. My own personal experience as a Zen priest, talking to practitioners suffering traumatic loss, is similar to that of the Episcopal Church bishops.

This discussion about grief, emotion and relationships is very important, as something traders forget or don't even realise is the *relationship* they enter into when they trade. Some may think they are forming a relationship with the market, but they are actually having a relationship with themselves. The market exposes the real you, the one full of attachments that create all your pain. Zen believes relationships can be one of our greatest teachers. Eventually the realisation occurs that it is not the actions of others that create the discomfort being felt, but rather the ideas and perceptions one has about a situation. Another reason to listen to the wise advice of the Buddha and discover for yourself who you truly are. Attachment obstacles close your mind and cause losing trades.

Attachment takes many forms and in fact can be associated with things that are *formless*.

A formless attachment is when someone is attached to something that lacks a physical form, such as an idea or an opinion. Consider the formless attachment to intelligence. A person may be well educated or very experienced in one career or field of information. If they are questioned, challenged or proven incorrect, they can become very defensive or evasive. They lack the ability to admit they were wrong or to simply say, "I don't know." The philosophy of *don't know* is fundamental in Zen and an important one in trading – something I will address in a later chapter.

Some people are attached to their intelligence, thinking, ideology, or opinions. Because of those attachments, they find it difficult to consider other ideas or possibilities. Albert Einstein, one of the greatest thinkers of all time, knew this and stated, "No problem can be solved from the same level of consciousness that created it." There is also this beautiful quote from the famous Zen teacher Shunryu Suzuki: "In the beginner's mind, there are many possibilities. In the expert's mind, there are few."

Regarding your perspectives about trading – you cannot be mentally flexible or come up with another brilliant idea if your mind is attached to the one it thinks it already has!

A trading example of formless attachment would be a stock you are considering to trade – one you were confident would be a winner. After much technical and fundamental research, you regard it as a sure thing, but the trade turns against you and reaches the price at which you intended to exit the trade. You don't act because you are attached to your original decision, your formless mental opinions about the stock. A lot of mental suffering is happening now. The bottom line is you are not accepting the reality of the present moment: the stock price is now at your previously pre-determined point of exit. *You are attached to how you wanted things to be, rather than acknowledging how they are.* Your actions are governed by what you believe and want: to be right and to make money. You cannot entertain the reality that you are wrong and suffering a loss.

ZEN DETACHMENT OPENS YOUR MIND TO WINNING TRADES

Buddhism has a long history of encouraging debate and open-minded thinking among academics and intellectuals. In some Tibetan traditions, it can take monks 20 years to attain the level of *Geshe,* which is similar to a university PhD qualification. The humility of these people is profound. Before any discussion or debate, one of the first declarations made is that they know little and that any opinions given by them should be met with rigorous challenges! If only our politicians and religious leaders were so non-attached to their ideologies.

With the considerations above, perhaps you are now seeing the similarities between trading and Zen. We know that trading is really just an idea, and the ideas we have about trading affect our performance. If we are attached to our trading ideas, we lack the ability to be flexible in mind.

If traders have inflexible minds, they find it difficult to consider other ideas – to see the merit in an alternative approach. Zen is asking you to empty your mind of your obstacles of attachment; to allow new possibilities and ideas to enter your consciousness. A mind ready for anything – a flexible mind without expectation – is the trader's greatest asset.

Being a non-religious belief system, Zen doesn't teach the concept of hell. Instead it teaches that suffering is caused from forming attachments. If, because of your conditioned thinking, you expect your life and those of others to be a certain way, I suggest your life will be quite hellish. If you are attached to your trading concepts, losses, wins and outcomes, then your trading life could also be hellish. The correlation between your attachments in life and your attachments when trading is 100%.

To trade well, you need peace of mind. To get peace of mind, you need to learn detachment. Hell, for traders, is here on Earth and it is populated by those who are attached to the way they want things to be – not addressing how they are in the present moment.

Pete's personal trading story

MY FIRST TRADING experience was as a teenager and apprentice tradesman. I bought beaten-up cars, and repaired and painted them to raise money to buy my first property. (My dad was a property investor and told me the share market was too risky, a fear I had to overcome.)

I liked spray painting and was good at it. I would make these cars look great in preparation for sale, but I had a problem when selling. I was attached. I remember feeling great resentment if the buyer offered a lower price. Eventually, if a deal was done, I would stand on the road and watch the car being driven away until it was out of sight. Only once I could no longer see the car did a feeling of satisfaction arise in my mind, generating the motivation to buy another car.

I was to revisit these feelings much later in life as a trader. Often, when needing to exit a trade at an undesirable price, I would have to accept the price I got and let go of the price I wanted. I learned to adopt the healthy practice of deleting the stock from my watch screen and portfolio – thus enabling my mind to move on to another trade.

The following is a famous and fun Zen story about an academic who is attached to his ideas, knowledge and education (formless attachment), and is therefore unable to listen and consider another's view:

A ZEN STORY

A university professor went to visit a famous Zen master. While the master quietly served tea, the professor talked about Zen. The master poured the visitor's cup to the brim and then kept pouring.

The professor watched the overflowing cup until he could no longer restrain himself. "It's full! No more will go in!" the professor blurted.

"This is you," the master replied, "How can I show you Zen unless you first empty your cup?"

—

CHAPTER SUMMARY

- Detaching doesn't mean you stop feeling.

- Unhealthy attachment creates obsession and a desire to over-control.

- You can be attached to an opinion as well as a physical object.

- Learning to detach opens your mind to see the boundaries and limitations that your mind creates.

6

THE ZEN SECRET
TO DEVELOPING
NON-ATTACHMENT

*I*f you continually want things your way, and that doesn't happen, you will most likely suffer mental anguish.

Consider these questions about life:

- Is it probable that in your life you will get everything your own way?

- Do you have a 100% win rate on all your life decisions, or have you experienced mistakes and loss?

- Do you expect that your life will be mistake-proof, perfect, and a continually smooth ride?

- Is it likely that everything in your life will turn out as you wish or prefer? What is the probability of that?

And these questions reframed for trading:

- Is it probable that in your trading you will get everything your own way?

- Do you have a 100% win rate with your trading or have you experienced mistakes and loss?

- Do you expect that your trading will be mistake-proof, perfect, and your portfolio equity will rise in a continually smooth way?

- Is it likely that everything in your trading career will turn out as you wish or prefer? What is the probability of that?

PERCEPTIONS CREATE SUFFERING

Experienced Zen practitioners will say that the secret to Zen is simple. It is our conditioned and inflexible minds that make it difficult. Experienced traders will tell you the same about trading.

Unhappy people tend to complain rather than having gratitude and seeing the positive side of a situation. Because their minds are inflexible, they tend to focus on what they perceive as wrong, and not on what may be right. Most traders do something similar: they react rather than respond. Zen masters are renowned for their non-reactive responses to most circumstances in life.

Reactions (as opposed to responses) while trading often come from lacking a solid plan. Moreover, as previously discussed, many traders cannot stick to a plan even if they have one. Reacting inappropriately is the problem. Traders do not realise that they are not just reacting to the market, but actually reacting to their mind's perception and non-approval of the current situation. They are not detached from whatever event is happening in that moment. Instead, they are more attached to a possible outcome, even though most outcomes are unknown. They have not learned to separate uncomfortable emotions from the present circumstance. To alleviate their uncomfortable emotions, they react. Reacting nearly always means breaking their trading rules in an attempt to alleviate their mental suffering.

So why is it so difficult to detach, and to sustain a position of non-attachment – to stay calm in the face of adversity? To not get upset, worried, angry, disappointed, depressed or anxious?

It is because our minds have been conditioned to think in a certain way. Zen Buddhists call that way *dualistic thinking*.

DUALISTIC THINKING IS THE GREATEST CAUSE OF TRADING WINS AND LOSSES

If you can stop habitually thinking in duality, you can develop the skill of non-attachment.

Dualistic thinking means we perceive objects and ideas as dualities: in *twos* (or sometimes in numbers greater than two). Examples of dualistic thinking include the mental concepts of tall and short, fat and thin, good and bad, stupid and smart, capable or incapable, rich or poor, male or female, black or white, up or down, right or wrong. They are all judgements and labels that we give things, and then *attach* to because of our minds' conditioning.

We lack the ability to observe and just *see* without judgement. We habitually give our observations a name – and that name is related to our judgement of the situation or object.

IT IS JUST AS IT IS

Zen philosophy regards everything *just as it is*. It is our thinking that creates the duality, and therefore the separateness, of everything. Habitual dualistic thinking (which is the way most people are raised to think) trains the mind to expect things to be a certain way. We have habitually learned to judge and label everything, then make assumptions, often without knowing the full facts of a situation.

If one maintains this view of separateness, of dualistic thinking, one comes to believe that things are always opposing each other, or always different. Everything becomes either less or more, you versus me, us and them, can't or can, why or why not, yes or no, up or down (to name just a few). Dualistic thinking is the reason people see things only in *black and white*. They lose the ability to realise the possibility of *grey*. In reality the colour grey is created from the combination of black and white, not from keeping the two colours separate. Another outcome is the inability to *read between the lines*, because in the fixed mind, things are only one way or another: they have to be, because they've been judged and named. Attachments to those judgements soon take hold.

Now, this philosophy of *just as it is* can get tricky!

You may be thinking that some things or people really *are* fat, thin, tall, short, good or bad. Portfolios *do* go up and down, some people *do* have terrible luck in their lives, etc. Yes, I agree these things are true. However, we all have different opinions about more or less everything, and these depend on our mental conditioning, developed from a combination of nature and nurture. For example, my height is 170cm; in Australia that is below the average of 179cm and on the short side. In many Asian countries, I am considered average, or even tall. So, am I short or tall? Different people have different mental conceptions, and therefore different expectations, depending on their conditioning and what they are used to.

I am old enough to remember racial segregation. As a child, I lived in Papua New Guinea. On Saturday nights, indigenous locals were not allowed inside the fenced-off enclosures of outdoor movie theatres. They could only watch at a distance, through gaps in the wire or perched in the nearest trees. That segregation was considered justified at the time, but would be unconscionable today. These rules no longer exist, so what has changed in this situation? Only mental concepts have changed; the people are still black and white.

Why is it that some find a person attractive, but others do not? Is the person attractive, or aren't they? Who or what is the judge of attractiveness? Why are large people considered attractive in some cultures, yet in other cultures it is the opposite? These opinions are the result of mental conditioning; to name and judge and think in duality.

Why does one trader see a falling market as an opportunity, while another sees a major concern? One trader reacts prematurely and sells their holdings at the first sign of a fall; the other holds until their method tells them to exit, or even goes in to buy, if that is their plan. Another trader places a buy in the market at value points, to take advantage of the premature seller. Some traders short sell (a strategy to profit from falling prices), taking advantage of the panic that may set in and produce further selling. These thoughts and actions are the result of mental conditioning; to name and judge (opportunity, value, catastrophe) and think in duality. The reality is that none of the above traders know what will happen, but the majority will expect themselves to be right.

To be a competent trader, you need to uncouple the mind from its pre-conceived concepts: judging and naming, or dualistic thinking. Habitual dualistic thinking is often caused by over-analysing, or obsessively thinking about what's right, creating an overwhelming desire to attain control. Developing awareness of dualistic thinking creates flexibility of mind. Thoroughly understanding the concept of duality makes us realise that we are the ones creating the friction in our minds; not other people, objects or situations. Market volatility is a consequence of traders' minds flip-flopping all over the place; one day bullish, another day bearish. You need to become aware of your dualistic thinking, and attain the awareness that your mind is moving as much as the market – in fact usually more!

The duality in your mind creates the market you see.

Perhaps now you are starting to understand the Zen philosophy that everything, absolutely everything – be it a concept about the physical (such as fat and thin) or a concept about the non-physical (such as good or bad) – only exists because of our perception; because of how our minds perceive. The mind often disregards other possibilities. For example, when I trade, I often ask myself, "Am I seeing what I have been conditioned to think and believe, or am I seeing what is actually happening?" This question helps me to uncouple my thoughts from my habitual dualistic thinking and consider other possibilities.

We – or more precisely our thoughts, coupled with habitual dualistic thinking – create and then name an object or subject, thus producing a personal level of significance.

It is our desire to have things the way we think they should be that makes events so significant to us. Most often, if situations are not the way we think they should be, or how we want them to be, we feel great suffering.

ZEN THINKING CAN CURE THE MENTAL PAIN OF ATTACHMENT

I mentioned in a previous chapter that one of the most extreme examples of attachment is war. Two sides, often arguing over an ideology, are prepared to kill each other to be proven right. The Buddhist view is that people are killing each other over an idea devoid of logic: how stupid is that? An idea that is empty in the first place, but is given significance because of our attachment to certain beliefs.

Some Buddhist practitioners become distraught when they witness the amount of suffering in the world being caused by attachment to concepts and ideas. It is often the accepting and letting go of this witnessing of suffering (their own as well as others') that launches the practitioner into *nirvana* (or enlightenment), or simply wisdom.

Traders suffer a similar frustration, often witnessing what seem irrational and unpredictable situations in the markets. They feel the need to be correct, to find reason, to predict and judge outcomes. However, it is the accepting and letting go of those needs that launch the trader into the next level of mastery.

Trading mastery, like nirvana, is not a place or thing, but a state of mind. A state of mind developed from an understanding of how easily the mind becomes attached to so many things – all because the mind has the habit of defaulting to dualistic thinking, of needing to give all things a name, and then a judgement.

Reflecting again upon this core teaching of Buddhism, that suffering is caused by attachment to all physical and non-physical things, we need to be aware of our conditioned mind and the way it thinks in duality. This is the key to a peaceful mind. Ultimately, what good is it to learn Zen, if not to be free from suffering and to be happy? Or, from a trader's perspective, to be calmer and more effective, and finally stop the mind from self-sabotaging via a lack of awareness, causing us to continually lose in the markets?

Pete's personal trading story

I REGARD THE following as my best ever trade, one of extreme detachment: it was a big loss. In the very early days of my trading, I subscribed to many advisory newsletters, one of which was written by an infamous Sydney stockbroker. "Mr R." was mostly a fundamental trader and he was advising clients to buy a stock called Pasminco: a zinc, silver and lead miner/producer. I followed the advice and bought a large parcel – 20% of my portfolio, far too large for my portfolio size. The stock fell and Mr R. advised buying more, so I bought another 20%, now holding 40% of my portfolio in one stock. The stock continued to fall. Mr R. continued to recommend it.

My account was getting smashed. Although a novice trader, I knew something wasn't right. The stock was trending down, and I had enough trading education to know what to do. I had to let go, detach, accept what was, and sell. I hit the *sell* button, taking a large loss on my trading capital.

The stock continued to fall to zero and eventually delisted, worth nothing. Although I took a large loss – one of my largest ever in trading – I learned one of my biggest lessons and had enough capital left to keep trading. If I had held on, not accepting what was, but wanting a different outcome, it would have almost wiped out my trading account and I probably wouldn't be writing this book.

The following story is an example of a Zen master's non-attachment to the naming and judgement of others:

A ZEN STORY

The Zen master Hakuin was praised by his neighbours for living a pure life. A beautiful Japanese girl whose parents owned a food store lived near him. Suddenly, without any warning, her parents discovered she was pregnant. This made them very angry. The girl would not confess who the father was, but after much harassment at last named Hakuin.

In great anger, the parents went to the master. Hakuin's reply was simply, "Is that so?"

When the child was born, the parents brought the baby to Hakuin, who was now viewed as a pariah by the whole village. They demanded that he take care of the child, since it was his responsibility.

"Is that so?" Hakuin said calmly, as he accepted the child.

A year later the child's mother could stand it no longer. She told her parents the truth: that the real father of the child was a young man who worked in the fish market. The mother and father of the girl at once went to Hakuin to ask his forgiveness, to apologise at length and to get the child back again.

Hakuin was willing. In yielding the child, all he said was, "Is that so?"

—

CHAPTER SUMMARY

- Dualistic thinking is the greatest cause of attachment.

- Being unaware of your dualistic thinking causes attachment to take hold.

- Wanting things to be only the way you would like them is a sign of attachment.

- To avoid attaching to objects and ideas, remember that everything is just your perception, often caused by habitual thinking.

7

THE OBJECTIVE OF ZEN

*I*f there is an objective of Zen practice, it is to create happiness, or at least to remove suffering and produce a level of contentment.

Let's look again at the first two statements by the Buddha:

1. Life is suffering.

2. The cause of suffering is attachment.

If the cause of our suffering is attachment, what is the antidote? It would seem to be detachment; so how does one detach?

What exactly are we detaching from?

Reviewing again the theory of dualistic thinking, when we have an initial thought, we attach a second thought (or more) to the first one. We firstly think of something, and then we secondly think that it is good, bad, wrong, right and so on. We may see a person we find attractive, and then thoughts and judgements follow, such as: they are lucky, vain, rich or unapproachable. We may be jealous, depressed, regretful, feeling anxious, thinking about loss etc. These thoughts could have another emotional component too, perhaps eliciting a physical response. Dualistic thoughts develop into being either pleasurable and desirable, or distasteful and preferably avoided. In the latter case, we are now suffering.

Suffering often creates a desire to act; to implement an action that will reduce or eliminate the mental pain. Action can come in different forms, but normally we act either mentally or physically. We might act mentally by taking a side, or a view, such as judging the situation as *right* or *wrong*. We may act physically, implementing control by deciding to avoid that attractive person or by removing ourselves from the situation. However, rather than resort to a control tactic to relieve suffering, what if we implemented the Buddha's strategy of non-attachment – and simply observed?

If we have thoughts of only observation – such as, "There is a person many would consider attractive," and do *not* attach our dualistic thinking to the initial thought, we avoid the suffering. There are no longer the challenging emotional reactions, nor is there a need to control or avoid. If you examine all the thoughts you have, you will notice that you habitually attach more thoughts of judgement – ones of like or dislike – to your first thoughts. If this pattern of thinking persists, it's not too difficult to see that reasonably quickly you will be suffering – or at least confused, distressed or possibly overwhelmed.

Is it possible to transfer those ideas of non-attached thinking, to disregard unfounded assumptions and to cease applying negative judgements and labels in our trading?

THE OBJECTIVE OF ZEN IN TRADING

Having set objectives and goals is an important component to successful trading. One critical goal to be attained is the ability to trade the stock market with minimal stress. The stress and mental suffering that many traders experience are the biggest obstacles to trading mastery.

If there is one thing to be achieved by implementing Zen in trading, it applies to the second sentence in the paragraph above. More than anything else, it is most definitely the mental suffering of traders that hinders fluidity of thinking. The mental suffering experienced by most traders is often attributable to overthinking, reacting instead of responding, and at times even panicking – which often results in over-trading. Over-trading is one of the most common reasons for underperformance – a mistake to be avoided.

What is really required is less thinking and more awareness.

Zen masters and experienced Zen practitioners claim that ultimate knowledge and expertise cannot be attained from thinking alone. In fact, the overuse of thinking is discouraged in Zen.

Non-attachment to thinking is encouraged in order to develop the skill of observation.

Often (or perhaps occasionally) you must have felt a situation wasn't *right*; it just didn't feel OK. There was a gut feeling or an intuition, despite which you proceeded with the action your thinking governed. Later, your doubts were proven correct. You somehow knew something was amiss. We are so used to applying learned logic, analysis and critical thinking that we find it difficult to detach from those thought processes and allow the possibility of an unexplainable *knowing*.

This may sound unscientific and speculative to you – but consider another question I ask myself frequently while trading: "Am I seeing what is happening, or am I seeing what my thoughts are making me think and feel?"

The concept of an ineffable *knowing* is not exclusive to Zen. This knowing can be enhanced by the Zen practice of detaching from critical thought so as to allow another view. That is the view of observation without judgement.

ZEN THOUGHTS ABOUT
WESTERN THINKING

Particularly in the West, we are all taught to think critically. Descartes's statement, "I think, therefore I am," could well be the gravest disservice to expanded thinking for humankind. It completely discounts the possibility of intelligence beyond critical and cognitive thought.

The examination of thought is the premise for many modalities in Western psychology. Those experienced in the field of psychology will know that Cognitive Behavioural Therapy (CBT), if not being replaced, is at least accompanied by many other modalities aligned with Buddhist and Zen teachings. For example, Acceptance and Commitment Therapy (ACT) is a model based on the Buddhist philosophy of accepting the present and then committing to a new path: a path with an end goal guided by a pre-set plan.

An example of ACT in practice would be an insightful trader accepting that his or her current method is not working, then making a commitment to a new method. Perhaps more importantly, the trader has attained a greater realisation and acceptance; also, the recognition that it is neither the market nor the method that is the obstacle, but rather their thinking accompanied by attachments of how they want things to be.

Dialectical Behaviour Therapy (DBT) is another modality used in psychology – one that focuses on skills such as accepting, finding meaning for and tolerating distress, with emphasis on bearing pain skilfully. These skills cannot be attained if the person is judgemental of either the self or the situation. The ability to detach from thoughts of fear – the fear of loss and the fear of missing out – is the greatest skill a trader can develop. It is almost comparable to the elimination of the fear of death, extraordinarily exhibited by the Japanese military culture of *Bushido*.

Thinking your way out of a situation often doesn't work; accepting *it is as it is* does.

Acceptance doesn't mean approval of the situation but it dissolves the obstacle of disapproval, allowing the mind to see an alternative response. Developing skilful means is an age-old Buddhist philosophy. When trading, you need to be very aware of how your mind is thinking and what habitual thoughts it is continually generating.

For example, Figures 7.1 and 7.2 illustrate two different ways of thinking about a trade: one with extreme attachment to price action, the other with observation only – no judgement.

Figure 7.1: Attachment to price action

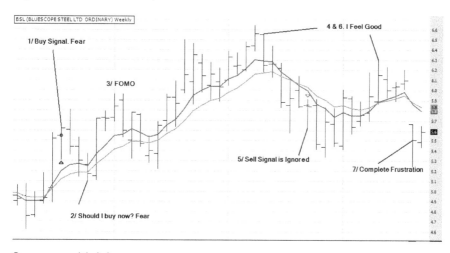

Source: wealth-lab.com

The above shows a stock trade from a simple weekly trend trading system. The buy signal is when the price makes a 52-week closing high, and the sell is when the weekly 7 exponential moving average (EMA) crosses below the weekly 12 EMA.

The conflicting thinking (and so reaction) of many traders is like this:

1. They hesitate on the buy signal and wait because of the strong up bar, producing fearful thinking because they judge and label the price as too high; they promise themselves they will buy if it pulls back.

2. They hesitate on the second chance to buy because the price is falling; they judge and label the situation as dangerous, producing fearful thinking that the stock will fall more, despite the fact they promised themselves they would buy if this happened.

3. They buy late in the trend, reducing the potential profit of the trade. After not buying the first or second time, their action is now fearful, thinking they are missing out on a good trade (FOMO). They berate themselves for not buying earlier; they judge and label themselves as being an incompetent trader.

4. They feel great because the stock is rising and the trade is in profit. They possibly feel justified in making the right decision; they may congratulate themselves with thoughts of being brave and resilient.

5. They feel bad because the trade is showing a sell; they are only at break-even because they bought late at thought 3. They do not sell, hoping it will go back up to where it was at the previous highs. They judge themselves for being wrong, or the market for being bad, or the system for not working, and make many other negative assumptions.

6. They feel good here, because the stock is rising again; they are pleased they did not take the sell signal at thought 5, even though they know they are not following the system they promised themselves they would. Somehow, an unexplainable ill feeling exists.

7. The stock gaps down well below the sell signal. The trade is a loss because they bought late and sold late. They feel incredibly stressed and frustrated. They realise if they had stuck to the system, acting quickly on both the buy and sell signals, the trade would be a small profit, not the big loss that it is.

They are now faced with the decision of what to do. Some sell; many don't and hold the trade, possibly for years as it continues to fall, forever reminding them of how bad a trader they are.

Instead of the trade being a small winner, they lose money, lose confidence, feel frustrated and confused, and look to something or someone to blame – often themselves. They may look for another method, one that 'works'. Their psychological problems around trading are compounded. It's a painful and expensive lesson.

Can you see how all the problems created for these traders have nothing to do with the market, the system, the stock, other traders, market commentators, indicators, volume, insider trading, auto-trading robots or anything else?

Now look at the next trade, with a Zen mindset.

Figure 7.2: Zen mindset

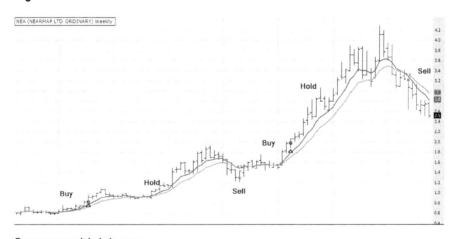

Source: wealth-lab.com

Trend trading is simple: it requires you to buy a stock that is rising and hold the trade until the sell signal is given. Any thinking about alternative possibilities is generated by you, not the trade. In the example above, using the same system, the Zen trader takes the buy signal, holds the trade until the sell signal is produced and then sells.

The process can be repeated if need be. This particular example is of a weekly system, but the time frame is irrelevant to the mastery of mental processes required. Whatever your chosen time frame, the skill that needs to be attained is one of pure observation, accompanied by detachment. This will help you stick to any method.

Fearful and judgemental thoughts will definitely come into the mind, but are not necessarily acted upon. They are recognised for what they are: a collection of reactions to lots of names and labels.

Fearful thoughts are not controlled, squashed, called bad, good, useful, non-useful, or given any other judgement or label. They are just thoughts to be observed – thoughts that are normal for any person operating in an environment with an unknown outcome, such as trading.

Zen masters have fearful thoughts too. The difference is they recognise the thoughts for what they are, allowing them to pass without negative judgement or unnecessary action.

No degree of mindfulness, as discussed in the next chapter, will help the over-thinking and reactive trader. We may be mindful of price fluctuation, and sometimes too much mindfulness of that can be detrimental, but what is more effective is detachment – non-judging, non-labelling – and the recognition of your habitual and damaging dualistic thinking. Those skills will help you follow simple processes designed to generate profit.

Pete's personal trading story

In 2004, I was asked to do a trading presentation at a traders' club near where I lived on the Central Coast of New South Wales, Australia. At the end of the night, I was approached by three men who had formed a research and development group using back-testing software. Two were full-time traders, the third a computer software coder. They all had great computer and coding skills, far better than mine. However, I did have the most trading experience. We worked together for a number of years, developing some great systems and managing to make some money as well. The lead up to the GFC was on and markets were strong, so the trend was definitely up. However, there was a problem with all of us – we couldn't stick to a method. It was then that I first identified the second big problem traders have: lack of commitment to a method. The four of us, despite our combined intelligence and experience, were still not making the money we could have. There was something severely lacking in our mental approach to trading. We wouldn't (or couldn't) stick to our designed methods because we had not learned the skills of detachment and observation without judgement.

A ZEN SAYING

If it is not necessary to do anything, it is necessary to do nothing.

—

CHAPTER SUMMARY

- In trading, it's not what you think; it's how you judge and label your thinking.

- The method or market is not the obstacle. Thinking, accompanied by attachment, is.

- Acceptance doesn't mean approval of the situation, but it dissolves the obstacle of disapproval, allowing the mind to see an alternative response.

- Fearful thoughts should not be controlled, squashed, called bad, good, useful, non-useful, or given any other judgement or label.

- Zen masters have fearful thoughts. The difference is they do not judge or label those thoughts. This keeps the mind from becoming reactionary, allowing a more measured response.

- The measured response is often *do nothing* – for example, hold the trade because it is not giving a sell signal.

MINDFULNESS
ALONE IS NOT ZEN

WHAT IS MINDFULNESS?

MINDFULNESS is being alert to what you are thinking; it is the first requirement in developing mastery of mind. If you walk out the front door on your way to work and forget to take something (keys, wallet, purse, sunglasses, phone etc.,) you are not being mindful. The reason is simple: your mind was distracted by thinking about something else. You might defend yourself here and exclaim, "But I had so much going on that morning. The kids were screaming, my partner was stressed, I was running late, my phone was ringing and the dog was barking!" However, mindfulness is the ability to focus on the task at hand and not allow your mind to be distracted. This is a skill that many of us need to learn, as it does not often come naturally.

Many people live their lives in an unconscious state of mind. They allow distractions to dominate their thinking, being unable to hone in on one or two tasks at a time and stay focused. Their minds flip from one thought to another. They allow their surroundings to distract and stress them, resulting in forgetfulness and lack of focus. This state of mind is what many Asian meditation teachers call the *monkey mind*. Perhaps a more familiar comparison for those of us in the West would be a puppy dog. Puppies, like monkeys, have a short span of attention.

They follow their noses – a new smell here or new smells there – and their direction and focus change continually, unless they are trained.

Becoming mindful is first developing the awareness that you have a pattern of distracted thinking and then learning to change it.

A ZEN STATE OF MIND

When you become mindful of your thoughts, your ability to focus improves. However, this may not necessarily make you a better trader or person. I am sure you know someone who is highly intelligent or capable – perhaps a teacher, academic, scientist, pilot or surgeon; but is that person emotionally intelligent? Do they have mastery of their emotional mind? Perhaps the person you know does, but we know that this is not always the case – so why is that?

The answer is they have not learned detachment.

Being mindful is a great skill – indeed a necessary skill to be a good trader or Zen practitioner, but it needs to be accompanied by the ability to recognise your dualistic thinking, the key to learning detachment.

Consider this scenario of mindfulness versus detachment:

Today is a trading day for you. You wake early and go for a walk, do some meditation, eat a healthy breakfast and sit down at your computer. Before the market opens, you check the overseas markets and notice they are up. You run some scans using your software, check alerts – you are focused and feel calm. You are mindful of your actions.

The market opens and it is down. You are surprised, as it's not what you anticipated. You start thinking it will be a bad day. You have just labelled the market as *bad* and lost complete awareness of how you are thinking. You do not buy the trades you intended. The market is bad, so you sell the trades you intended to keep.

At lunchtime the market turns and rallies. Your original analysis was correct: the trades you could have bought at a lower price on the open have gone up. The trades you sold at a low price have turned and risen above where you sold. Opportunity has been missed and profits given back. You feel stressed, frustrated, foolish and regretful, and later hear that a politician made a negative comment about interest rates which caused a short-term market reaction. You are angry and judge the politician an idiot – a label that also proves incorrect when it is later discovered that she was just taking advantage of a situation for personal political gain.

Even though you were mindful of your actions, you missed observing yourself judging and labelling the market. It was *bad*. Your mind *attached* to the thought *bad* and got you worried and nervous. You went into damage control mode – a mode that was unnecessary and not part of your original plan.

Now let's replay that scene with a Zen state of mind.

Today is a trading day for you. You wake early and go for a walk, do some meditation, eat a healthy breakfast and sit down at your computer. Before the market opens, you check the overseas markets and notice they are up. You run some scans using your software, check alerts – you are focused and calm. You are mindful of your actions.

The market opens and it is down. You are surprised, as it's not what you anticipated. You are perhaps disappointed, but are aware of how you are thinking and feeling. You watch the market with a mind of interest and curiosity, not one of judgement and labelling. You buy the trades you intended and hold the trades you planned to keep because you are committed to following your method.

At lunchtime the market turns and rallies. Your original analysis was correct: you find out later a politician made a negative comment about interest rates which caused a short-term market reaction. You smile to yourself, realising once again that the market is prone to short-term reactions that it is often best to ignore.

IF THERE IS A SECRET, THIS IS IT!

I hope you picked up the most important point from above:

You watch the market with a mind of interest and curiosity, not one of judgement and labelling.

If there is a secret to Zen, this is it!

Reflect back on the story of the Zen master accused of fathering a child. Hakuin never reacted, but said only, "Is that so?" He knew that reacting in that moment was a waste of time; better to let things play out on their own, as no amount of interfering from him would change anyone's mind. He never judged or labelled anyone or anything.

Reflect also on the previous Zen saying: "If it is not necessary to do anything, it is necessary to do nothing."

If the struggling trader described above had a set of rules, there was nothing to do but follow those rules. If the trader did not have a set of rules, they were experiencing the first problem of unsuccessful traders: not having a method.

If they did have a set of rules and a method, they were experiencing the second problem in trading: they were not sticking to those rules, and that was because they allowed their mind to attach to a negative dualistic thought – in this case, the judgement of the market as *bad*.

In reality the market was neither bad nor good. It was doing what markets do: going up and down, reacting to the constant stream of information affecting it. In fact it is not the *market* reacting. Many traders fall into the trap of thinking the market is something it's not. The market is not an entity of itself; it is just all those other traders attaching and then reacting to the constant assault of information they are receiving. This includes robotic and mechanical systems that react to the information of changing prices or other indicators.

YOU CAN HAVE A VIEW, BUT NOT AN ATTACHED ONE

The danger of judging and labelling anything in the market is that it fixes your view. Traders need flexible thinking – not fixed views.

Of course, at times it can be very profitable to have a view. For example, you may hold the view that gold will rise, and so you add gold positions to your portfolio.

But the judgement and label of, "Gold is in a bull market and I won't consider it otherwise," reduces flexibility of the mind. If gold falls and you don't sell, or you double up because of your conviction and it falls further and your losses increase, those actions come from your attachment to your opinion about gold.

The non-attached trader will sell, or even reverse positions (go short), when things do not go the way they first thought. Those traders can change course quickly because there is no attachment to the original analysis: "Gold is in a bull market." There is nothing wrong in having a view of the market reached from good analysis. Problems arise when the mind is attached to its view, reducing flexibility of action. Being mindful and focused during changing situations is a good skill. However, there is no escaping what is required to become the second and more flexible trader discussed above – the trader with a Zen state of mind. To be like this, one needs to learn and recognise the dualistic thinking of the mind.

The ability to stand aside and observe not just the market action, but also your thinking, is one of the most powerful trading skills you can develop.

> ### *Pete's personal trading story*
>
> SOME YEARS AGO, I was coaching a client who had reached the pinnacle of his professional career. This person's intelligence was without question. However, from the beginning I noticed a strong emotional bias to many decisions about trading, which I found quite amazing considering his personal achievements.
>
> I later received a phone call during market open hours. The client was quite emotional and concerned about the price action of the market that day, which had created an undesirable effect on a portfolio of stocks. At the same time, he was in a life-threatening situation at work. After some ranting about the market, the question came: "*What do I do?*"
>
> I paused to reflect on my Zen training, then said, "You turn off your screen, forget the market for the time being and focus on your task in the present moment."
>
> The situation ended safely, but I never again heard from my client; perhaps he did not appreciate my direct approach.*
>
> * Almost 10 years later, and just before the publication of this book, I reconnected with this gentleman. He is still trading and with more success – a testament to his dedication in overcoming his personal challenges.

A ZEN STORY

Two monks stood observing a flag moving in the wind. One argued the flag was moving, the other the wind.

A Zen master approached, and they asked, "Master, does the flag move or the wind?"

"Neither," came the reply. "It is your mind that moves."

84

CHAPTER SUMMARY

- Becoming mindful is first developing the awareness that you have a pattern of distracted thinking and then learning to change it.

- Watch the market with a mind of interest and curiosity, not one of judgement and labelling.

- The ability to observe your thinking is arguably the most powerful trading skill you can develop.

9

BEING IN CONTROL AND SUPPRESSING FEAR IS NOT THE SOLUTION

THE title and content of this chapter may surprise you, because often you will hear the opposite statement about trading. Many still believe that to be a good trader, you need to control your emotions. I couldn't disagree more. What is required is *emotional recognition*. My belief is that this skill is more common among women and hence the reason they can outperform men at trading.[2]

The ability to first recognise your emotions and then understand them is the key to trading well. Supressing emotions only creates confusion. You need to understand your emotions so you can develop a strategy to deal with them. Women seem more able to name their feelings, which makes it easier to identify their thinking, thus enabling the clarification of their emotion.[3] Men are often confused by their emotions because they lack the ability to name and then understand them.

By now, you may be realising that awareness of your thoughts, which is followed by not attaching to those thoughts, is the key to peace of mind. Peace of mind is a requirement of trading well. A judgemental

---

[2] 'The Role of Hormones in Financial Markets' (University of Leicester, 2016).
[3] 'Gender Differences in Emotion Regulation: An fMRI Study of Cognitive Reappraisal' (National Library of Medicine (US), 2008).

and attached mind will often make fearful and thus illogical decisions – a scenario we must avoid if we are to be successful in the long term.

- Recognising fear and not suppressing it will allow calmness and peace of mind to increase.

- Recognising fear and not suppressing it will allow you to trade better.

I use the word *allow* because nothing in Zen is forced or controlled. Realisation, calmness and peace of mind come to those who stop controlling or forcing things to happen.

FLOW, BUT SOMETIMES FIGHT

Let me give you an example of how recognising – but not suppressing – the mind's thoughts can work in an aggressive or chaotic environment. As a youth, I studied karate and some other Eastern martial arts. I also tried boxing, a fighting modality more common in the West which focuses mainly on two things: attack (punch) and defence (block), with the occasional duck and weave.

Eastern martial arts focus on very similar things – attack and defence. However, there is a huge tactical difference – at times, step out of the way and let the force of the opponent pass by you. Do not attack, do not defend; if you can, do not fight – in fact, do nothing! Also, if the opportunity presents, use the force of the attacker to your advantage. Do not lose the advantage of thinking clearly. Stay calm and refrain from becoming reactive and filled with fear or rage.

This philosophy can be used in trading. Often when trades go against them, traders feel the need to do something. However, have you realised that the decision to act comes mostly from the desire to alleviate your unpleasant feelings? Suppressing fear, ignoring it and thus fooling yourself that you are in control, prevents the realisation that you are just *reacting* to fear and not managing it. This is the opportunity for you to use fear as the tool it can be: the tool of realisation.

Fear is not to be discarded or suppressed as a worthless and inconvenient emotion.

NO MIND

If you have not seen the movie *The Last Samurai* starring Tom Cruise as Captain Nathan Algren, I recommend you watch the wonderful scene where he is learning to fight with a wooden sword. He is repeatedly defeated, until he embraces the advice of a Samurai onlooker: "Use no mind." The captain realises he is overthinking his technique, thus creating anger and frustration within himself. When he stops attaching to the thoughts of getting it right or wrong, he starts to flow with his opponent and then his own blade. He doesn't so much win that one fight (he and his opponent draw), however he experiences an awakening to the fact he has been limiting his own ability through his desire to be in control. This *no mind* is the beginning of his mastery.

It's a wonderful example of a strong, capable man with incredible drive and willpower, stepping away from his mind's desire to control and get things perfect. Once he allows those thoughts to be in the background, focuses on being present in the moment and flows with the battle, he gains success.

So, if controlling our emotions is not the answer, what is?

SUPPRESSING FEAR IS THE TRADER'S GREATEST TRAP

A misperception about Zen accomplishment is that by controlling the mind, no fear will be experienced. Let me assure you this is far from correct.

In Zen, awareness of fear, accompanied by detachment, is what's encouraged. Western thought is centred around avoiding or controlling the emotion of fear. Zen is asking us to do quite the opposite – in fact it wants us to do something radical: turn towards fear and embrace it!

This theory is not so radical when we consider the reasoning for it. Awareness is a powerful tool. If we do not look at which emotions are driving our decisions, how will we ever discover why we keep repeating the same life mistakes or self-sabotaging our trades? Zen asks you 'not to avoid' your thoughts, feelings and actions, but to look at them with a mindset of curiosity and willingness. This can be very challenging.

I have witnessed people physically run out of a meditation retreat when asked to sit still and contemplate their actions in life. The feelings arising from realisation overwhelm them, so they run away from the challenge of more awareness and insight.

Often, it is not easy to consider questions that the enquiring mind may produce. These challenging thoughts and life questions that arise could include:

- Why am I in this marriage?
- Why am I in this job that I hate?
- Why don't I say what I feel?
- Why do I feel I live a life of quiet desperation?
- Why do I compulsively shop?
- Why do I overeat?

- Why do I drink as much as I do?
- Why do I gamble on sport so often?
- Why do I have so much anxiety?
- Why do I have depression?
- Why do I watch so much pornography?
- Why do I stay stuck and refuse to act for positive change?

These are tough questions.

At a meditation retreat, you are asked to stop your habitual thinking and actions, to give your mind the time and space it needs to open and reflect. Reflection will make you aware of the questions and answers you avoid – then of course sometimes it becomes so challenging you want to run, like some do.

Traders run all the time, except instead of running out of a meditation retreat, they run from the market. Or they run **to** the market, to escape their unhappy lives, like I did.

Traders also need to have an enquiring mind. Our actions as traders are often a mirror of our actions in life.

At some stage in your trading career, you will need to ask questions like the following:

- Why don't I buy?
- Why can't I hold a trade?
- Why can't I sell?
- Why do I constantly screen-watch?
- Why do I trade so often?
- Why do I constantly change my mind about the market and trading?
- Why do I hide my performance from those who might help me?

- Why can't I follow a method without constantly interfering with it?

- Why don't I stop trading and take a break to reassess my method?

- Why can't I ask for help?

- Why do I hide my performance from my spouse or colleagues?

- Why don't I spend the money and time to get some training, learn that new software and approach my trading in a much more business-like manner?

These are tough questions. If you have attended trading lectures, I am sure you have been advised to stop your habitual trading (thinking and actions) so as to give your mind the time and space it needs to open and reflect.

However, you don't do these things, because you are stuck in a pattern – a pattern you seemingly can't break away from. If this is the case, you may have an addiction to trading.

If you do muster the courage to stop and reflect on all these personal and trading questions, the answers will be hidden among...

FEAR

Fear of the outcome if you act. Fear of loss if you make a mistake. You fear that if you leave the job you hate, you may not get another, or will have to settle for one that pays less. If you leave that unhappy relationship, you fear you may not be able to meet anyone else, or you may fear the emotional or financial pain of starting over. You may fear the challenge of learning something new, such as the trading course you have been thinking about or some back-testing software you have avoided buying. You may fear the emotional confrontation and pain of in-depth counselling and treatment to cure your anxiety, depression or addictions.

Your fears are so great, you do nothing. You are like a rabbit in the headlights of an oncoming car.

Paralysed.

Most of all, though, the following are the fears that govern traders' actions:

- Fear of loss.
- Fear of missing out.
- Fear of losing a profit

How are you feeling? Are alarm bells ringing, as I expose to you how you may think and feel and what the problems may be?

Unfortunately, it gets harder before it gets better. Until you realise and accept that the negative emotions and patterns in your life will be repeated in your trading, you will never be successful at trading.

ZEN AWARENESS WILL FREE YOUR PAIN AND ANXIETY

What is required is the ability to recognise fear and neither attach to it nor avoid it. Developing that skill will provide the calmness and peace of mind required to perform consistently well – not just at trading, but in any endeavour in life you choose.

Fortunately, there is a solution to all this – the Buddha's fourth Noble Truth:

There is a method (system) to achieve the end of suffering, a way to be calm with peace of mind.

A Taishin Shodo Zen story (Taishin Shodo is my ordained name)

AS PART OF my training, I attended a five-day silent meditation retreat facilitated by an elderly monk of a Tibetan tradition. During the retreat, upon request we could have a private audience with him. I regarded myself as reasonably experienced; I had been meditating for 25-plus years, had lived in a monastery for two years and was in training for Zen ordination. I had a burning question in my mind: how do I and others overcome fear? I entered the monk's small room, bowed in respect, as tradition expected, took my seat and asked my question. Without hesitation, the answer came: "Turn towards it. In fact do more than that. Put your arms around it and embrace it for what it is: part of you. It is you. The longer you continue to run and avoid fear, the longer it will remain your enemy. The moment you welcome it in and serve it tea, it will become your friend." In trading, and life, we never stop learning.

A SUFI SAYING, WHICH IS ALSO ZEN.

You yourself are your own barrier – rise from within it.

Idries Shah, leading Sufi thinker of the 20th century.

CHAPTER SUMMARY

- Develop the skill of emotional recognition.

- Give your mind the time and space it needs to open and reflect.

- What is required is the ability to recognise fear as a thought, then neither attach to it nor avoid it.

- Suppressing fear is the trader's greatest trap. Awareness will free you.

- Nothing in Zen is forced or controlled.

10

THE ZEN SYSTEM
FOR PEACE OF
MIND AND PROFIT

REMEMBER the Four Noble Truths?

1. Life is suffering.

2. The cause of suffering is attachment.

3. It is possible to end suffering.

4. There is a method (system) to achieve the end of suffering.

The fourth Noble Truth is the theme of this chapter.

What is this system the Buddha claimed he had discovered?

TO TRADE WELL, YOU NEED A PEACEFUL MIND

Let's review the correlations we have identified between trading and life:

- Trading and life are not easy. At times both involve loss, suffering and sometimes even tragedy.

- You can't always get what you want, either from trading or from life.

- Being human, whether we trade or not, we often look for ways to escape our suffering by adopting avoidance or unhealthy coping strategies.

- Being human, we fear an unknown outcome.

- Less can be more if we let go of the need to always be in control.

- How we think, particularly becoming aware of our dualistic thinking, can be paramount to our perceptions about trading and life.

- Intense emotions can be an asset, not a liability. It's not logical to discard or ignore our assets.

- Watch the market and life – particularly others' actions – with a mind of interest and curiosity, not one of judgement and labelling.

- Detaching doesn't mean we stop loving, feeling joy, being sad or experiencing any other emotion.

- Detaching can expand our thinking and reduce self-imposed limitations.

- Fear is often the root cause of our difficulties in both trading and life.

- Zen masters have fearful thoughts too – the difference is they do not judge or label those thoughts. This keeps their mind from making quick assumptions or becoming reactionary, thereby allowing a more measured response.

From the points above, it would seem that if you are not calm, with a peaceful mind, it is difficult to perform well in the uncertain and at times chaotic environment of the stock market – and also the chaotic environment that life can be.

As traders and participants in life, we need to learn to be calm, accept that we work and live in an uncertain environment, and let go of the need to know the outcome.

As I mentioned at the start of this book, good performance in any profession requires theory and practice – that is no different in the system the Buddha developed.

FIVE OF THE SIX *PEACE AND PROFIT* RULES

From a Zen perspective, here is the theory part of the system.

There are five theory rules – and some of them you probably won't like.

1. Refrain from killing.

2. Refrain from stealing.

3. Refrain from lying, gossiping or any false speech.

4. Refrain from sexual misconduct.

5. Refrain from intoxicating substances.

In addition to these, the final and sixth rule is the practical part of the system, which brings it all together, and that rule is: meditate (to be covered in the next chapter).

Before you reel back in horror and think you are back at church, the temple or Sunday school, consider the objective we are wanting to achieve: *to be calm, with peace of mind.*

FOLLOWING RULES KEEPS YOU ZEN

The five rules above are what Zen calls the Five Precepts. If you are serious about becoming chilled as a trader and person, then it is the starter pack in cleaning up your act. Zen – unlike many religious, philosophical or belief systems – puts the responsibility completely on you by using the word *refrain*. There is no, "Thou shall not…" How you trade, and how you live, is your choice. As a trading teacher, I can point the way to what works; then you can decide whether it suits you.

As a Zen teacher, I do the same.

SOME LIFE EXAMPLES OF THE FIVE REQUESTS TO REFRAIN

1. Most of us don't go around killing. However, there are times when you condone it by your actions – for example, buying a nicely packaged piece of steak from the supermarket. I am not saying you can't eat meat; I am pointing out the subconscious approval of an action you may detest. If you were required to perform the act of killing another living being with your own hands, would this change the choices you perhaps now unconsciously make? Apart from the moral side of this discussion, there are the health factors. We have all read the science: we know a diet low in meat and high in vegetables, fruit and grains is better for the body and mind.

2. Most of us don't go around stealing. However, there are times when you may unconsciously or consciously condone it. You may notice the checkout clerk at the store makes a mathematical error in your favour, so you say nothing. Your colleague is away the day your boss praises the team for an ingenious idea, and you neglect to point out it wasn't your idea, but your absent colleague's. You log in to a subscribed website using a friend's username and password to avoid the joining fee. You take a car park space that's allocated for disabled drivers, and you justify it by thinking it's only for a few minutes.

3. Most of us are not consistent liars, but we bend the truth to avoid emotional confrontation. We don't disclose our trading errors to our partners and we only talk about our wins to our colleagues, failing to mention we have a dozen losing trades sitting in a hidden account. Our retail therapy expeditions seem surreal; a ballooning credit card balance is hidden from our partner. We complain how things are organised at our community event, but we won't offer to help or even make constructive suggestions. We gossip about others and are negative and critical of them; it's a way of avoiding responsibility for our own struggles and frustrations.

4. Many of us are faithful to our wives, husbands or partners. However, many are discontent and either wish for something else or constantly planning and thinking about escape. Women are likely to look for emotional gratification outside their relationship. Men are more likely to lust over other women, have affairs, go to prostitutes and massage parlours or have a pornography addiction. It's easier to masturbate as we visualise another than to disclose our true feelings and frustrations to our partner, therapist or close friend. Our partners are either objects of security, physical attraction or habit. We may feel sexually inadequate or emotionally frightened, so we avoid genuine intimacy; we may not even know what that is or really feels like. We go to the stock market to feel stimulated – to feel anything – because inside we feel empty. Winning and losing, at least we feel connected to something, even if it's painful.

5. Most of us like a drink and it can feel like a reward after working hard. Alcohol can calm the nerves and enhance your ability to relax and socialise. Sometimes, one drink becomes three and suddenly you are drinking every weeknight and more on weekends. "It's okay, I'm only a social drinker," you justify to yourself. One or two won't hurt; some drink a lot more than you. You drink a lot, but you think you are high-functioning. If you are young, you may take a pill or two at a party or a

rave. You know it's not wise to drink with pills, so instead you top up with a couple of smokes of marijuana or some cocaine. You live or work in the city and have a corporate job; your colleagues drink every night, maybe even at lunch – it's part of the job. The morning meetings are in the café downstairs. It takes two strong shots to get you going, plus quite a few more through the day. You drink alcohol to unwind and coffee to wind up. You live with constant thoughts in your mind and you are either reactionary or mostly unconscious of what you say or do. Your focus is poor and you lack awareness, particularly self-awareness. You have heard the terms *presence* and *flow*, but have never experienced either or really understood what they are.

IMPORTANT CORRELATIONS BETWEEN TRADING AND ZEN

One financial market's movement is correlated to another. What happens in the US affects European and Asian markets. Comments by world leaders can move a stock market or a currency. Global growth increases demand for oil, driving up oil stocks and other growth sectors of the economy. Uncertainty increases *risk off* mentality and can produce a flight to gold and gold stocks. Interest rate cuts can result in demand for financial and property stocks. How one market performs and reacts affects another.

A trader's performance is correlated to their lifestyle. What we eat and drink affects how we think. Our lying, selfishness and unhelpful actions can produce feelings of confusion and disconnection. The excitement and emotional rollercoaster of an affair produce guilt, indecision and stress. Other avoidance techniques in our personal lives produce similar unhealthy emotions. Our coping strategies and addictions lead to financial difficulties, applying even more pressure to our fragile sense of identity. Without honesty and integrity, we can become frustrated, angry, confused and either controlling or reactive.

To trade well with consistency, we need calmness and peace of mind. To attain that state, we need awareness of our thoughts and feelings. It's difficult to be aware of our thoughts and feelings and be aware of dualistic thinking if our physical and mental being is coping with stress from all angles. Coherence is the key to calm. When different markets are coherent and without conflict, they perform in a consistent manner. When a trader's personal life is disciplined, honest, structured and healthy, it is reflected by consistent trading results.

I acknowledge that refraining can be challenging, but if you want performance, consider how dedicated professional sportspeople are. They know it takes discipline, hard work and a combination of theory and training before they get to enjoy the rewards of winning. If you want to trade like a Zen master, you need calmness and peace of mind. To get peace of mind, you need to be like the disciplined and successful sportsperson. Apply the effort of discipline to Zen theory – do this by adopting the Five Precepts.

For your mind to appreciate your efforts of understanding and adopting the theory, you also need to train. Similar to the professional sportsperson's physical training, meditation is your training and practice, and this will be discussed in the next chapter.

Pete's personal trading story

DURING 2007 I was using trend trading systems on a weekly time frame. I was also trading aggressive momentum systems, developed a few years before with my research and development group. The markets were hot and the profits were flowing. However, my trading was still erratic and unstable – a reflection of my mind. I had separated from my partner of 20 years, and I was living alone in a beachside unit. My father was gravely ill, and I had the responsibility of being his physical and financial carer. I was still feeling emotionally burned from a property deal that I lost money on two years before. I was single, somewhat sour and sore at the world. I threw myself at the markets, grasping for my identity, and started to revenge trade. I spent many a night (in Australian EST time) trading the gold market when the US and London markets were open. I used one-minute charts to increase my trading frequency. I could be up A$10,000 one night and down the same the next night.

I was leveraged up at least ten times my annual average income, often more. I remember having an anxiety attack as my account fluctuated wildly on a volatile market day. A severe anxiety attack feels like a heart attack; it's very frightening. One night I lay on the floor in a semi-foetal position, crying "I just want to go home," knowing quite well it wasn't a physical home I was yearning for, but an emotional home. My feelings of sadness, joy, identity and confidence were correlated to my account balance. After a winning streak, I would suit up, drive my cute little white Mercedes to my local upmarket bar, and be *the man*. Chat to the girls, buy drinks for strangers, be happy and confident.

During my losing streaks, I would stay home or walk the beach to curb my depression, and ask myself, "There must be a better way?"

My medium- and long-term trend trading accounts were winning, but my short-term impulse trades were dragging my accounts down – and me with them. I wasn't well and I knew it. The most frustrating thing was that despite all my knowledge, intelligence, experience, workshops, coaches, study, hard work and wins, I felt like shit.

The following quotation is from Alan Watts, a British writer and speaker. Despite his personal challenges, he has been attributed with interpreting and popularising Zen Buddhism. Watts was a heavy smoker and in his later years, drank heavily. He died in 1973 aged 58.

A ZEN SAYING

No one is more dangerously insane than one who is sane all the time. He is like a steel bridge without flexibility, and the order of his life is rigid and brittle.

—

CHAPTER SUMMARY

- To trade well you need a peaceful mind.

- Your trading performance is correlated with your personal life.

- The more honest, structured and disciplined you are, the more benefit you will have in your life and trading.

- Following a good life system, such as Zen, is like following a good trading method: neither is perfect, but each provides structure in uncertain environments.

11

MEDITATION, THE ZEN SYSTEM'S MOST IMPORTANT RULE

*A*LL good methods have a theoretical component. However, theory on its own is not enough. To master a method, theory needs to be combined with practice. With regard to the method of Zen, the Five Precepts are the theory and the sixth and final rule of the system is the practice: meditation.

Meditation is the *practical* part of the system of Zen.

The practice (method) of Zen is similar to a trading method – but either method is useful only when implemented. Without implementing your trading method for a period of time, you won't know how it performs and whether it suits your personality. You can't make money sitting on the sidelines and avoiding the trading work of buying/selling and the resulting emotions. One of the greatest challenges of trading is to let go of the eternal search for certainty and face your fears – and conduct the process of trading. We realise that to have profit, we must trade (although at times we don't feel like it).

To be successful at trading, we simply must trade.

The person who avoids meditation is similar to the trader who won't diligently trade. Without meditating for a period of time, you won't appreciate the benefit of following the Five Precepts or come to appreciate how doing so (or not doing so) will affect your personality. You can't reach a state of calmness and peace of mind by avoiding the work of meditating; nor can you expect to experience the emotions and realisations that only meditation produces. One of the greatest challenges of Zen is to let go of the eternal search for certainty and face your fears – and go through the practical process of meditating. We realise that to have calmness and peace of mind, we must meditate (although at times we don't feel up to it).

To be successful at Zen, we simply must meditate.

COMBINE DISCIPLINES FOR PEACE AND PROFIT

I believe that one of the most beneficial exercises you (or anyone) can do to improve your trading results is this: no matter how experienced you are, you should select one method only and trade that method diligently and consistently for a period of time. Keep good records of profits and losses and of how the trades performed. During the trading exercise, it is also important to keep notes regarding your emotions and reactions. This procedure of testing, measuring and analysing will do more for your trading than any course, book, lecture, podcast, YouTube video or possibly any other training modality. In recent years, trading simulators have become a popular teaching tool. However, simulators do not produce the emotional intensity of trading live and having skin in the game.

For example, you could trade a system for a period of one year – a system that is designed to be analysed weekly. Stick to it, record it, gain/feel the experience and discover/record how it expands your knowledge and thinking. Your method may be totally systematic, discretionary or largely governed by economic fundamentals. It could be a combination of all those qualities. Once you have chosen a method, trading your method is the only way you can assess how it works and feels for you. A simple system with only a handful of rules, applied diligently and patiently, will obviously produce results. It will also produce an inevitable moment of realisation. That moment is what a trading colleague of mine calls the *Ah-ha!* moment. Every trading student I have taught – and I am not exaggerating when I say every one of them – has had the *Ah-ha!* moment. This is the moment they understand that trading is a process – a process that unfolds *if we get out of the way and let it be.*

Often after some time in the market (this could be years), aspiring traders will contact me with their questions. Some of those questions are technical, but many are about their suffering related to trading experiences. This marks a moment of realisation: the moment they realise they need something else – something more than just technical knowledge.

That something more is calmness and peace of mind.

I believe one of the most beneficial exercises a person can do to improve their understanding of Zen is this: strive to implement the Five Precepts *and* meditate regularly. It is the combination of both theory and practice that produces the result of a calm and peaceful mind.

Trading discipline and Zen discipline require a similar approach. The rules are simple – stick to them. Do your best to refrain from the things in your life that will obstruct your mental clarity. Apply the rules of the Five Precepts and then enhance that mental clarity with meditation. The more you introduce the Five Precepts into your life, the easier it will be to meditate. The more you meditate, the easier it will be to follow those precepts.

Remember that the actions and results in your life outside of trading will correspond with your actions and results within trading. Trading and life are correlated. A good, simple trend-following system, applied with Zen discipline and patience, compounds capital over time and rewards you with big profits.

The system of Zen will do the same for your life. It will compound the positive qualities and negate the negatives.

Here are some of the benefits of the ancient practice of Zen meditation. Do you think these benefits would help you trade?

- Higher self-esteem and self-trust, leading to better overall relationships.
- Gaining wisdom and clarity of mind, with improved concentration.
- Increased inner strength and better decision making.
- Reduced mental chatter/busy mind (monkey mind).
- A sense of youthful happiness and openness to life.
- The healing of chronic depression and anxiety.
- Marked improvement with sleeping.
- An ease of dealing with previously difficult situations.
- Reduced chronic stress.

THE BONUS OF RULE SIX: TRADE AND BE HAPPY

There are extraordinary claims about how meditation will improve your life (which includes your trading prowess). So, it is important to examine the concept of meditation. The practice is designed to make us aware of habitual thinking – this alone can improve our trading. As a bonus, it can also lead to increased happiness. After all, we all started trading to improve our lives. If meditation will improve our trading *and* make us happier, we get double the return on our investment.

When you slow the mind's chatter via meditation, that simple process allows a vital skill to develop: the ability to become aware of the chatter.

An example is when you listen to an infant who is just learning to talk. The child is relatively incoherent and babbles away because he or she can. You listen patiently, and perhaps with amusement, discerning the information you hear and not taking it too seriously.

If you can consciously be the observer of your own mind's prattling thoughts, you (your full consciousness) will become the master. The mind can become a student. By becoming an observer of your thoughts, you can also become an enquirer, gently questioning thoughts that are often formed from past conditioning. You can now begin to gain insight into your mind's processing techniques and how to improve them, thus becoming calmer, wiser, less reactive and more effective. By just noticing a thought and not attaching to it, we become observers of our thinking processes. By not attaching any meaning, conclusion or judgement to the thought, we can then start to detach from our conditioning – thus becoming more able to see an alternative view. This newfound awareness gives the mind an open and unlimited view, allowing more insight to arise naturally and emotional suffering to decrease.

Now we will discuss the trick to mastering meditation – as many find it difficult.

LAY THAT TOOL DOWN AWHILE

Humans have an incredible asset that animals do not have: a large, intelligent brain. This organ can be our greatest asset and our worst liability. Our brains are problem solvers and designed to think. We could call the brain a tool; if used well, it is the best tool we have in our possession. Once a problem is solved, we should ideally lay that tool aside – no matter how temporarily. But many people and traders never do lay that tool down. They overuse it by brooding over the past and worrying unnecessarily about often-unlikely consequences of the future. They are addicted to *thinking* and pay a price for that addiction

– by never experiencing peace of mind or calmness. They can never be truly happy.

Meditation is a rest from mental work. When we meditate, there really isn't anything to do except wait patiently for thoughts to subside, while remaining alert and passively aware. I mentioned animals, and I will make a comparison to a state of mind: that of alert animal awareness. Imagine an antelope grazing passively in the forest, calmly aware of its surroundings but ready to flee at the first sign of danger. When the action of flight (if needed) is over, it returns to its state of calm with alertness, continuing to graze, but ever ready to respond if necessary.

Meditation teaches us to use the mind in a way that many perceive to be the opposite of the mind's job. Most regard thinking as an end in itself, rather than merely a means to an end. The best way to use the mind is to apply its logic to a problem, then put that logic aside and rest in calmness and peace of mind – similar to the antelope's ability to return to a state of calm alertness.

CARNEGIE'S FOUR STEPS: A WESTERN EXAMPLE OF LAYING DOWN THE TOOL

During my childhood, my mother identified me as a worrier. She herself was prone to the same affliction. My mother gave me a book to read: *How to Stop Worrying and Start Living* by Dale Carnegie (Richard Clay, Ltd, 1948). I still remember Mr Carnegie's four-step process of meditative problem solving:

1. Identify the problem or what it is that is worrying you.

2. Collect all the information you can about the matter. That simple step can often solve the problem. If it does not, it then gives you options which lead to step 3.

3. From the information and options gathered in step 2, decide your course of action.

4. Whatever the decision, stick to it! Set a time frame for your decision, then revaluate the situation when the time is up.

In his early career, Mr Carnegie was a night schoolteacher. He noticed a pattern of thinking among his students. The worriers struggled to progress in their studies and lives. The students who did not worry as much progressed with more ease. To help others, he wrote the book mentioned above – one of the first modern self-help books.

The four-step process described above is an example of using the mind as a tool of logic, then applying a very sensible process. A similar process can be used to develop a logical and simple trading system – such as the one described in Chapter 3.

When I present and teach Carnegie's four steps to trading students, most agree that step 3 – deciding the course of action – is quite challenging. However, by far the hardest is step 4 – sticking to the decision. Step 4 is where the thinking mind does not want to stop. It does not want to let go of its coveted job of processing and working to keep solving, looking for more or looking for better. It wants to keep you safe, but at this stage of the process letting go and letting be is what you require of the mind. Decisions and plans take time to evolve and to produce results. You can no doubt now understand how hard it is for many traders to *let profits run*, because trading requires your mind to let go and let be. By all means do your analysis, but once you decide upon a trade, act on that decision – after that, there is nothing else to do. Well, actually there is! Stop thinking about it: let go of the thinking and let the trade be. Put the tool of logic down. If you can't learn to do that, you will sabotage the trade by interfering in the logical process that you probably spent much time and money developing!

At this point, Zen meditation picks up where Dale Carnegie left off.

It is well known that trading attracts intelligent, analytical and logical thinkers. No wonder they struggle with step 4. Applying Zen to your trading is asking you to accept, stop, let go, let be and cope with the unknown. Allow the process of your plan to unfold. That is understandably a very difficult thing to do when many have been conditioned to stay in control, to make frequent decisions or to micro-manage a situation.

Dale Carnegie developed a great idea: use the mind's logic to formulate a plan. He was a businessman and knew that plans are imperative to success. Trading is no different. However, he didn't realise how hard it is for many people not to fall back into worry mode and then experience the temptation to change their plan, rethink ideas, second guess, micro-manage, constantly watch, focus too much on what others are doing or saying, meddle unnecessarily or keep analysing into a state of analysis paralysis. These people need another form of training apart from logic – or even willpower.

They need meditation.

NEUROSCIENTISTS MEET ZEN

Neuroscientists at Harvard University have conducted experiments using MRI scans, finding that meditation can lead to the brain's prefrontal cortex thickening in certain areas – improving the performance of higher brain functions. They also found that the amygdala, sometimes called the brain's fear organ, begins to shrink, reducing stress-induced overactivity.[4]

In his *Essays in Zen Buddhism*, Professor Daisetz Teitaro Suzuki describes levels of mental states. He makes comparisons between

---

[4] sitn.hms.harvard.edu/flash/2013/mindfulness-meditation-a-mental-workout-to-benefit-the-brain

meditation and what happens when we are in deep sleep. During deep meditation, there is loss of consciousness that is indistinguishable from deep, dreamless sleep. The difference is, when we are asleep, we are unconscious and unaware – but when in a meditative state, our minds are relaxed but still aware.

So, when we meditate, we attain a state of awareness like that of a kind of *super-antelope*: calm, less affected by external stimuli, but ready to act if needed. It is possible (in fact, I assure you, as I have repeatedly experienced and seen it happen) for regular meditators to become calmer, less reactive and increase their level of functioning.

WHAT THAT TOOL IS REALLY FOR

Conscious mental activity and logical thinking are the solutions to many of our problems and challenges – for example, developing a trading plan. However, misdirected thinking can at times can have a detrimental effect on our pursuit of happiness. Many would say that happiness is the ideal result achieved by the mind thinking – using its logic to create a successful outcome. Zen, on the other hand, says that happiness, ease and peace of mind come from the practice of laying down the tool of logic. You will find no better time to do this than during your meditation or after your decision to commit to a trade. This practice of *laying down* will result in two invaluable skills: firstly, you will be able to take the experience of meditative calm into your life and work; secondly, the mind's logic will be heightened by taking breaks from continuous thinking and overworking. It will become less burdened and free to cognise clearly – during your trading and in your daily life.

As a child, you had to learn to walk and talk. Many don't realise that you also have to learn to train your mind to be happy. The practice of putting down our thinking during meditation, while staying intensely alert and passively aware, reacquaints us with the peace of mind small children have. That feeling is sometimes called *bliss*. It is the wonderment a child experiences from a new experience. Bliss can be a state of mind without unhelpful thoughts such as unreasonable desires, expectations, anxieties and worries about the future: the types of thought that create a desire for excessive control.

The Zen way of life and meditation will acquaint you with profound calmness and peace of mind: results of allowing the tool of logic to rest of its own accord when not needed. This laying down of logic can be temporary – perhaps for only a few minutes a day, slowly increasing that time to an amount you feel is most beneficial to you. Some find it more constructive to meditate for shorter periods twice a day than for one long period. Experiment and you will find your preference. There really isn't anything to do in meditation – just rest from mental work while staying alert and passively aware, much like our fellow being, the antelope.

Pete's personal trading story

In 2016, I was offered Zen ordination. I felt I wasn't ready for such a commitment and needed more study and training, so I travelled to Taiwan and then on to Japan for a meditation retreat. One morning I was working alongside an elderly monk, weeding the temple paths. I asked a technical question about Zen, and he said to me, "See that weed in front of you? Pull it out." Undeterred, I asked another question, and the response was, "See that other weed beside you? Pull that one out too."

At that point I realised what he was attempting to teach me. Zen is not all about what you know, but how you might *be*. Trading is the same.

I then weeded in silence.

A ZEN STORY

Two monks, one senior and one junior, were travelling together. At one point they came to a river with a strong current. As the monks were preparing to cross the river, they saw a very young and beautiful woman, also attempting to cross. The young woman asked if they could help her cross to the other side.

The two monks glanced at one another, because they both had taken vows not to touch a woman.

Then, without a word, the older monk picked up the woman, carried her across the river and placed her gently on the other side. He then continued on his journey.

The younger monk couldn't believe what had just happened. After rejoining his companion, he was speechless. An hour passed without a word between them.

Two more hours passed, then three. Finally, the younger monk could not contain himself any longer and blurted out, "As monks, we are not permitted to touch a woman. How could you then carry that woman on your shoulders?"

The older monk looked at him and replied, "I put her down on the other side of the river hours ago. Why are you still carrying her?"

CHAPTER
SUMMARY

- Meditation is the sixth and final rule of the *peace and profit* system.

- It is best to combine meditation with the other lifestyle disciplines of Zen.

- One of our mind's greatest assets is its ability to think (and to solve problems).

- One of our mind's worst liabilities is its inability to turn off and rest; to put down awhile its desire to think, plan, cognise and deduce – often resulting in worry.

- Traders need to learn the skill of focusing the mind's power – to reason logically without the propensity to overthink – so that events can unfold without interference.

- Zen meditation can create an intensely intelligent alert mind, which is also peaceful and passively aware.

12

MEASURING PEACE OF MIND

*I*f following the Five Precepts and meditating develops our awareness, depth of realisation and levels of consciousness, and also increases the probability of succeeding in trading and life, how do we know if we are progressing well?

The logic of implementing (and sticking to) a trading method for a period of time is that results and performance can be measured. After the designated period, one can review and adjust the method and/or one's trading performance. This process of *test and measure* continues – hopefully a continued uptrend in performance is the result. This is a relatively simple process to follow as part of an overall strategy when trading. However, how does one measure performance of meditation or levels of awareness – especially if the goal is to measure levels of calmness and peace of mind in trading and life? What control or measuring system do we have at our disposal to examine such subtle modalities?

REALISATION IN ZEN AND TRADING RESULTS CANNOT BE FORCED OR CONTROLLED

The summary in Chapter 8 included the statement, "Nothing in Zen is forced or controlled." The power of Zen comes from being an observer, allowing events to unfold and not forcing your will upon a situation. You cannot force your will upon the market. However, the ability to decide what your response will be will depend on your level of consciousness.

In his book *Power versus Force* (Hay House, 2014), Dr David Hawkins explains the connection between individual levels of consciousness and human behaviour. He also asks the reader to consider where true power exists.

Dr Hawkins claims every decision we make and every action we take is driven by our individual level of consciousness. Hawkins takes the concept a step further when he scales the level of consciousness from 20 to 1000, proposing that the levels 700 to 1000 belong to people like the Buddha, Jesus and the poet Kahlil Gibran – to name just a few of the many notable historical figures that could qualify. Some well-known people who have recently lived or are still living – such as Mother Theresa, the Dalai Lama, Thich Nhat Hanh and Eckhart Tolle – could be included in this list. The lower levels on the chart are for the rest of us; aspiring towards a degree of enlightenment or at least developing calmness and peace of mind.

Figure 12.1: Levels of consciousness

	Level	Scale	Emotion	Process	Life-View
Power	Enlightenment	700–1000	Ineffable	Pure Consciousness	Is
	Peace	600	Bliss	Illumination	Perfect
	Joy	540	Serenity	Transfiguration	Complete
	Love	500	Reverence	Revelation	Benign
	Reason	400	Understanding	Abstraction	Meaningful
	Acceptance	350	Forgiveness	Transcendence	Harmonious
	Willingness	310	Optimism	Intention	Hopeful
	Neutrality	250	Trust	Release	Satisfactory
	Courage	200	Affirmation	Empowerment	Feasible
Force	Pride	175	Dignity (Scorn)	Inflation	Demanding
	Anger	150	Hate	Aggression	Antagonistic
	Desire	125	Craving	Enslavement	Disappointing
	Fear	100	Anxiety	Withdrawal	Frightening
	Grief	75	Regret	Despondency	Tragic
	Apathy	50	Despair	Abdication	Hopeless
	Guilt	30	Blame	Destruction	Condemnation (Evil)
	Shame	20	Humiliation	Elimination	Miserable

Looking at the levels above, it is clear to see that one needs to be at level 200 or higher to attain the calmness and peace of mind to perform well as a trader. I suggest many traders are around the 100 level. Operating from a level of Fear, their emotion is Anxiety, their process is Withdrawal and their life view is Frightening. With this level of consciousness, their trading will consist of emotions and actions such as being afraid to buy or feeling anxious if they have a trade open. Also, at this level of consciousness they are unable to commit to a method, at times panicking and selling early. They experience their trading as being incredibly frightening.

Comparing that reactive behaviour to the consciousness level of 250, which is only 25% of the maximum level of 1000, you now have a trader with a healthy Neutral level: who has Emotional Trust,

Releases into the Process and finds the experience of trading to be Satisfactory.

The way to raise your consciousness on the scale is to have a healthy lifestyle by applying the Five Precepts, then combine that lifestyle with meditation – the *peace and profit* system from Chapter 10. We know what predominantly causes our decisions when trading the market – emotion. Look carefully at the emotions, processes and life views of the person living in the Force section. That person will struggle to be Zen in the markets or in life itself.

I repeat, much is correlated: be Zen in life and you will be Zen in your trading.

In Chapter 7, I discussed the power of acceptance and the psychological modality of ACT. Acceptance is at level 350 in the consciousness scale. Acceptance is having the ability to accept *what is* and then committing to a plan of therapy or change. The trader with that power (true power, not force) is able to forgive his errors and those of others, mentally transcend the chaos the market regularly produces and work from a harmonious state of mind.

IMAGINE

In 1971 John Lennon wrote the song *Imagine*. The lyrics of the song request that people detach from material possessions and ideology to create a world in which they live in peace. Imagine how much calmness and peace of mind you would have if you could hover around the levels of 350 to 600. Imagine how successfully and smoothly you could trade and how happy this would make you in your life. Personally, I feel I swing between the levels of 100 to 600 depending on what is happening in my life. Also, very importantly, the level I operate from depends on how well I have maintained my lifestyle discipline – via the Five Precepts and regular meditation practice. An upswing on the scale could last for weeks or even months. I am thankful to say the downswings below 200, normally lasting a few moments or perhaps just a day or two, are fewer. Nonetheless, they do happen. Just as the market can be volatile, Zen teachers and practitioners are not immune to emotional volatility and down days. In case you are wondering, the times I feel around levels of 700-plus are when I am in deep meditation, perhaps participating in a Zen retreat or visiting a monastery.

However, you don't need to go to the extremes of Zen study and practice like I did. At your own pace, introduce the Five Precepts and meditation into your life.

In Dr Hawkins's scale, you will notice there are eight levels of Power and eight levels of Force. To get the most from your practice of the *peace and profit* method, I suggest you approach it with the qualities stated at levels 200–250. These levels ask that you have courage and neutrality, release your fears and trust the process. Such levels of awareness can be increased only when we cast our doubts aside and open our minds to what may be possible.

LEVELS OF CONSCIOUSNESS ARE NOT A NEW IDEA

The concept of measuring consciousness was explored many years ago by Zen scholars. A Zen priest by the name of Kukai (774–835 AD) wrote an impressive book called *Treatise on the Ten Stages of the Development of Mind*. Kukai was not only a Zen priest and scholar, but also an artist, engineer and dam builder. He was a man of many talents and founder of his own sect of Zen Buddhism. However, his treatise is considered by many to be his greatest work. The following list is what Kukai regarded as the levels of consciousness – levels that the mind develops as it moves towards achieving the ultimate understanding: enlightenment.

1. **Basic instincts:** the stage of the *human animal*, focused primarily on needs such as food, shelter, sex and physical safety.

2. **Morality:** one gains awareness about morality.

3. **Belief in a higher power:** one believes and relies upon supernatural beings. Often accompanied by the expectation of a heaven (or better life) beyond this world – thus gaining relief from present worldly anxieties. This stage applies to most religions, but not to Zen.

4. **Ego and attachment to identity:** one realises the effect of ego. An awakening about the effect of attachment to ego on their own personality and those of others.

5. **Cause and effect:** one realises that any action creates reaction – thus gaining a profound understanding of causation.

6. **Compassion:** one develops a non-discriminating compassion for all beings.

7. **Perception:** one understands and is enlightened to the fact that all thoughts and feelings are just the individual's perception.

8. **Oneness:** one realises everything on earth and in the universe, be it physical or non-physical, is connected. Or as the famous monk, the late Thich Nhat Hanh, described it: interconnected.

9. **Emptiness:** one realises that all thoughts, feelings, perceptions, impulses and even consciousness are only concepts, and that they do not exist. We give them an existential meaning. Emptiness also applies to physical things because everything, such as the creation of a physical object, either starts with a thought, an instinct or via causation.

10. **Enlightenment:** one fully understands the previous 9 stages, especially the 7th, 8th and 9th levels, and is then able to incorporate that understanding into every part of one's life.

Dr Hawkins and Kukai (who lived over 1,200 years earlier) came to similar conclusions. Supreme consciousness can be achieved simply by becoming a better person. You might ask, "What has all that got to do with mastering trading?" My answer is *"Everything,"* for it will be extremely difficult for you to trade well if you stay in the lower levels. And as mentioned earlier, that is when one is below level 200 in Dr Hawkins's scale and in the lower five levels of Kukai's scale.

I regard these levels as *states of mind* more than *levels*. For if we are able to remove all boundaries of thinking from our consciousness, levels cease to exist (that statement is level seven-through-nine thinking). With regard to attempting to allocate a fixed level to oneself or another, that's almost impossible. For we will always be sliding up and down the scale depending on our own circumstances and those of the people around us. However, as our consciousness matures, so does the ability to recognise and change our state of mind – hence not getting trapped at less useful levels for too long.

MORE *DHARMA*, LESS DRAMA

The changes in lifestyle that are asked of you and the commitment to meditation are not part of some sadistic Zen discipline or ritual. The purpose is for you to realise how much your habits distract from gaining awareness. Traders distract themselves from acting in a disciplined way because of the variety that financial markets can provide. We do something very similar during our daily lives, distracting ourselves with enticing temptations – for example, different forms of technology, sounds, food, alcohol, sex, drugs, chatting, gossiping, over-working or over-exercising. These are methods of avoidance. Avoidance from looking within and contemplating. Avoidance of often uncomfortable, but nevertheless valuable realisations. The observant reader may have noticed something about the Five Precepts: they are not designed to make life harder, but rather easier, by reducing the complications that create stress in our lives. They are also designed to make meditation easier. A less troubled mind is a product of a more disciplined lifestyle. This creates a less turbulent meditation – thus creating more awareness.

The Abbot of the monastery I lived in for two years had a favourite saying: "More *Dharma*, less drama."

He loved that saying so much he had it made into a bumper sticker. The word *Dharma* means "the teaching of Buddhism." So, we could translate the bumper sticker meaning to: "Follow the Buddha's system for peace of mind." To continue with the car analogy, think of the Precepts being the vehicle you're using on the path to true power, with meditation being the fuel.

A trading coach teaching well-constructed methods can elevate your understanding of process, bringing about an *Ah-ha!* moment regarding the markets.

A well-constructed method to attain peace of mind will elevate your level of awareness. A higher level of awareness will create a higher level of calmness and peace of mind, thereby improving your ability to trade well. Your measuring tool will simply be how you think and feel. The level of 350 produces a life view of harmony. At that level, you will start to feel more in flow with trading and life. Your stress levels will reduce and you will start to see opportunities you could not before – or didn't even think were possible.

Incorporating trading with Zen is not some genius mathematical trading system (combined with a secret power) handed down from an ageing master living on a mountaintop in Japan. It is a simple system of living a wholesome life to the best of your ability and then combining it with meditation.

Good traders adopt simple systems – simplicity and discipline. This is the key to success and profits.

Zen masters adopt simple systems – simplicity and discipline. This is the key to calmness and peace of mind.

So to be aspiring traders, we need to be aspiring humans. It is a full circle that we must always travel.

Pete's personal trading story

WHEN I FIRST started trading in the mid-1990s, I attended meetings at trading clubs and associations. I also participated in a number of trading courses. Attendees at these meetings and courses would mingle during the breaks. I noticed a question they often had for each other: "Are you in the market?" Many of these people had been studying the markets and trading for years. They seemed no closer to realising their dream of becoming a competent trader or investor – in fact, many had moved further away. I would search among the more experienced attendees in the hope of finding a teacher. No one seemed able to give me a process or definitive answers to my questions about what to do. They didn't seem confident of what they themselves were doing, or would say they were not in the market at that time and so couldn't help me. I detected a level of avoidance and perhaps embarrassment. It seemed they were trapped at a level of fear. Perhaps some struggled to impart their knowledge to others.

I would often leave these meetings feeling frustrated and confused, reflecting on the statistic that only around 5–10% of traders were successful. I would also reflect upon my training as a tradesman spray painter and then my teaching years of that same trade at college. There was a process I had learned and now a process I taught. There was no attitude of "Sometimes I paint, sometimes I don't." I wondered if the solution was the opposite of what most traders do. Perhaps the solution was to be in the market the majority of the time and have processes to follow. Processes of method and mind.

The Buddhist teacher Rinpoche Trungpa once said, "If you don't know anything about Buddhism, best not to start. However, once started, best not to stop!"

I believe the same philosophy applies to trading.

A Taishin Shodo story

ON MY PATH to ordination, I had many doubts about the power of meditation. Analysis, theory and discipline were fine. However, could I embrace the unknown to allow a possible transformative benefit? That theory didn't fit so well with my mind, which was attached to logic. Encouraged by a friend, I attended a meditation retreat facilitated by a meditation master who had completed extensive training and claimed to have extraordinary abilities, including the ability to transform thinking and raise consciousness with a single meeting. "What rot!" I thought. However, despite my doubts, I decided to proceed with the meeting. On my way to the event, I became aware of my judgemental thinking. I decided it would do no harm to put aside my doubts and participate to the best of my ability. I would neither accept nor reject my doubts, but stay neutral (level 250). Upon arrival, I was invited to do an *open eye* meditation with the master. It was a transformative experience to say the least. I had read books and heard stories about such experiences and, as I said, doubted if such things were possible.

What happened next was this: as we looked at each other, a tunnel formed between us. The best I could describe it would be a tunnel of light, or perhaps energy. It seemed as if an ultimate connection had been formed between us and she knew everything about me in a second. I felt emotionally naked and totally exposed. My personality mask was down and I was unable to hide anything about myself. I remember closing my eyes, shaking my head, looking about in an attempt to test or break whatever this was, but every time I returned to her gaze, it was there. An indescribable knowing, connection, peace, acceptance – even love. The experience seemed to last a short time, perhaps only a few minutes. It could have been much longer, but time didn't matter; it was the quality of the experience that did.

Many years later (and now with more experience), I understand what happened. When our minds totally detach (either through our own ability or with the assistance of another) from our self-imposed sense of self (ego), what is left is ultimate peace and awareness. This is true power, accessed via meditation. All of us have that power.

A ZEN DRAWING

The calligraphy Zen symbol of *Enzo*: the moment the mind is free to let the body/spirit create.

CHAPTER SUMMARY

- Trading results and Zen development cannot be forced.

- True power comes from implementing the Five Precepts and meditation.

- More Zen *Dharma* equals less drama in your trading and life.

- Raising your awareness will increase calmness and peace of mind.

13

IDENTITY, THE SELF AND EGO

*I*f you have read other trading books, I am sure you have come across the claim that ego is a big problem for traders. According to the *Oxford English Dictionary*, the word *ego* means self-esteem, self-importance, self-worth, self-respect, self-image and self-confidence.

There is a lot of *self* among those references!

Gained from my personal experience of 26 years trading along with over 30 years meditating and then Zen training, I believe that the mind negotiates between the conscious and the unconscious. Your perception of reality is then produced from this negotiating part of the mind. Upon performing that function, the mind then establishes a sense of personal identity.

ZEN ASKS YOU TO RECONSIDER
WHAT *IDENTITY* MEANS

Therefore, it would seem that ego is about the self and one's identity.

What if I told you that your idea of yourself and your concept of identity could be false?

This is a concept I would like you to consider. From the Zen perspective, you do not have a self or an identity, at least not as you may perceive it. That is a challenging statement for those of us who have been raised in a modern Western society: a society extremely focused on who you are, what you do and what possessions you have, thus creating the formation of an identity. An identity you are probably very attached to.

Perhaps, by now, you understand a fundamental Zen teaching: your concept of reality is in your mind and how you think. The Zen principle of self and identity is the same – it is only a perception of your mind. In our society, many are habituated to *do well*. This equates to having a well-paid job, owning an impressive house, driving a late model car, being with an attractive partner, experiencing regular travel and owning many other possessions to keep us entertained – all to provide a sense of fulfilment. When we engage socially with people for the first time, the question often arises (particularly from men), "What work do you do?" In the city of Sydney, where I frequently work, a common question is: "Where do you live?" Because it is now important to others (who assess our identities and make judgements about our social status) not only what your career is, but also what suburb you live in or what school your children attend.

I do not often tell strangers what I do for a living. I know they will make assumptions, which at times creates ill ease or begs more explanation. The answer, "I work in finance," normally kills the conversation! Conversations rarely start with more soulful questions, such as, "What do you do apart from work?" or "Are your parents and children well?" or "Have you seen a great movie or show lately?" Customarily, the focus of relating to another is about establishing an identity and securing one's concept of self. At best, probing questions based on identity and ego can be a poor conversation starter. At worst, they can create a sense of separation and self-righteousness, which are exactly the opposite qualities you need to be a trader – humility is more beneficial than ego.

From a Zen perspective, focusing on your concept of self and its *identity* will not produce calmness and peace of mind. We need to let go of the restrictive concept that our identity is tied to what we do, where we live and how much money we make. If we marry our trading performance to our identity, we will be happy when we win but we will be depressed when we lose. For example, when you hear about your friend and his trading losses, you may feel some pity for him, but it won't really bother you because his losses are not your problem. This is because his losses don't challenge your sense of self and identity. However, your own losses would likely challenge you greatly – a sign your ego is very attached to desired results.

STRONG ATTACHMENT TO A CONCEPT OF IDENTITY MAKES IT HARDER TO ACCEPT LOSSES

There is an objective in removing your ego and identity from your trading. When you trade and lose, your level of attachment to the undesirable result needs to be similar to the thoughts you had about your friend. You need to develop the same *not my problem* mindset about losing your own money. The trader needs to dismantle the association of self-worth with how much money they win or lose.

Zen philosophy is this: the mind wants to preserve whatever concept of identity it has about itself. It does this by clinging to the concept of the identity it already has, or else grasps at an alternative identity it believes could be better. This attachment to identity is what spiritual leaders like the Dalai Lama mean when they say that suffering is caused by "self-grasping ignorance." *Self-grasping* means you are unwilling to let go of the identity or ego you hold so dearly. The Dalai Lama is not saying you are an ignorant person, but that you are ignorant of the tricks the mind is playing, setting you up for failure by being too attached to your sense of self and identity.

Zen is not saying you shouldn't have goals or aspirations. Zen wants you to self-actualise. Zen alerts you to the fact it is the *attachment* to your concept of who you are that creates friction and therefore suffering in your mind.

The American psychologist Abraham Maslow developed the famous pyramid of human needs. He nominated self-actualisation as the highest level. The bottom level contains basic needs such as safety and survival. The mid- to upper levels include belonging and self-esteem – achieved via prestige and feelings of accomplishment. Many Westerners (and now Easterners too) have been educated to believe the pinnacle of accomplishment is a strong sense of identity gained from material or notable success. No wonder we struggle with trading, a pastime that can often create the challenge of unexpected loss – resulting in feelings of failure.

INTELLIGENCE ALONE WON'T KEEP YOU ZEN

Trading attracts intelligent, successful people. These people have made their way forward in life playing a certain game. That game rewards them for being intelligent and hardworking, learning what is right and wrong, then applying that to their profession. Often ego and a strong sense of identity, coupled with self-esteem and self-confidence, work well. In fact these qualities are necessities in many professions. Unfortunately, all that doesn't work in the game of trading. You can be a very intelligent, confident, hardworking person and easily fail at trading. Conversely, if you can separate your mind from your ego/identity/self, you do not need to be academically intelligent to do very well at it. If you have worked diligently to understand your ego and detach from what may be an unhealthy sense of identity, congratulations – you are on the path to becoming a master trader!

Here are some Post-it Notes I have above my computer screen to remind me to remain aware of ego:

- Smart people lose because the ego rules.
- Master traders lose at times.
- Master traders don't take losses personally.
- I, emotionally, accept losses.
- Master traders let go of the need to win.
- I don't need instant gratification.
- I don't need external gratification for internal worth.
- Trading is, at times, not about developing a better method – it's about developing a better mind.
- Emotionally attached traders create opportunities for calm traders.
- The most important thing you need is calmness and peace of mind.

I have many more such reminders among my notes, but these resonate with me the most. Detaching, accepting and letting go are some of the hardest qualities to achieve – not just as a trader but as a person. It is why I have stressed in previous chapters that you need to work on the person as well as the trading method.

I know some of you will still not be convinced, so I will show you how this can be put into practice in the next chapter.

Pete's personal story

AFTER A FAILED marriage early in life, I experienced my first bout of depression at age 26. My family doctor suggested I attend an assertiveness course at my local hospital, facilitated by health professionals (that course was followed up with a personal communications course). Something odd and a little profound happened during the first course. Most of the content being taught was about self-esteem, self-importance, self-worth, self-respect, self-image, self-confidence. There was a great deal of focus on doing and being what you wanted. The year was 1986 and the buzz word of the decade was *individuality*. A family man aged around 40 objected to the course content, saying it was too self-focused. "Life isn't all about me," he said. After a period of discussion with the facilitators, he decided to leave the course, never to return, shaking his head in disapproval. Most of the course attendees thought he was misguided, frustrated, perhaps angry and just plain wrong. I wondered if he was right. For even at my young age, I had noticed a trend among humanity. Despite our Western privileges, many of us were not happy and were often confused. Free thinkers like him were rare. Perhaps he knew his true self.

A ZEN STORY

A young monk approached the master and said, "Master, I am in deep peace and feel I am in a constant state of equanimity. I realise now all my mental afflictions, pain and suffering are not reality, but just in my mind."

After hearing this, the master used his walking stick to repeatedly tap the monk on his forehead.

The young man reacted and exclaimed, "Why did you do that?"

The master retorted, "You were saying?"

—

CHAPTER SUMMARY

- Zen asks you to reconsider what *identity* means.

- Attachment to the ego/identity/self makes it harder to accept losses.

- Intelligence won't help you detach; in fact it may hinder.

14

I WANT MONEY,
NOT ZEN

MANY years ago, when I first started teaching trading, at the end of my presentations I would ask attendees to complete feedback sheets. On one such sheet I received the comment, "Just teach us how to make money, no psychology stuff." Only a few months before I started to write this book, I taught a one-day seminar followed by my usual Q&A review session at the end. I asked the attendees whether they wanted to discuss Zen or trading psychology, or did they want to explore more technical trading methods? The overwhelming response was the latter.

If we reflect upon the statistic that only 5–10% of traders are successful, which topic do you think would have been more beneficial? I know from experience that many readers will have their doubts about how important it is to include psychology in their trading – particularly trading psychology from a Zen perspective.

Perhaps you have doubts about the value of Zen reasoning. Surely the way to profit from the market is to have a superior system, or to know something others don't. Perhaps the key to profits is a system that trades more often, so as to produce more opportunity. Maybe an automated system is the answer – one you can set and forget and just watch the profits flow into your account.

Have you ever thought to consider what emotions and attachments influence your thinking?

Or have you considered the emotions and attachments of the trading system developer? Another person who is creating the system they think you want (the system *you* think will make the frequent and easy money)? Have you considered what is involved, practically and emotionally, in trading a more dynamic, aggressive and frequent trading system?

A DAILY SYSTEM FOR THE NASDAQ

Let us look at a trading method – an income trading system – to explore the possibilities and see whether we can find some clarity to those questions in the previous section.

The system discussed below is at an intermediate to advanced level. To follow the concepts, it will help if you have knowledge of trading technical parameters. To duplicate the rules and run your own scans and tests, you will need back-testing software. I am increasing the technical level on purpose because stepping up to a more dynamic system requires the trader to be more experienced. Without that experience, it will be highly likely the trader will not succeed.

The system below is designed as an income generator. It produces a little over one trade a week and averages a return of 4.1% a month.

Let's first look at the detail and then discuss the pros and cons:

- Stocks to trade: the **Nasdaq 100** is the sector the system trades.
- Starting capital: **$100,000**.
- Position sizing: use **$20,000** per trade every time.
- Have a maximum of **five trades only at any time**.
- **Do not reinvest profits** to compound capital. Trading capital and trade size remain constant.

BUY RULES OF THE I-WANT-MONEY SYSTEM

- Check that the Nasdaq 100 index closing price is above its 13-day Exponential Moving Average (EMA).

- If the Nasdaq 100 index closing price is below its 13-day EMA, <u>do not</u> proceed to the next step.

- If the Nasdaq 100 index closing price is above its 13-day EMA, proceed to the next step, which is:

- Buy the opening price the next day if:

    1. the stock's closing price is the highest in 20 days; and

    2. the stock price is 8% higher than it was 20 days ago (so the stock is appreciating at an annualised rate of 100%); and

    3. the On Balance Volume indicator (OBV) is higher that it was five days ago.

TRADE SIZING AND SELECTION RULES

If there are more buy signals than you have the capital to purchase, give preference to the lowest-price stock.

For example, the system divides your capital into five lots, buying $20,000 trades using capital of $100,000. If you were in a hypothetical situation where the system was holding three trades worth $60,000, you would then have $40,000 remaining to buy.

The system may generate three buy signals on the same day, so how do you choose which ones to buy? You have enough capital to buy only two trades, but three signals are given. The answer is you buy the two stocks that have the lowest price, ignoring the third stock that signalled.

The three trades signalled may have prices of $79, $129 and $327. In this case you would buy the $79 and the $129 stocks, leaving aside the $327 stock.

Another case may be: you have remaining free capital of just $20,000 as the system is already holding another four trades – your capital allows a maximum of five trades. This time you would have enough capital to buy only one more stock and that would be the one with the lowest price, at $79.

There are two reasons why the system has this rule of favouring the lowest-price stock:

1. Knowing what stock to buy, because of a set rule, removes all bias from the decision-making process – and obviously makes the decision process simple. However, it has an added benefit. At a later date, when revising the performance of the system, evaluation is simpler because there has been no discretion used in the buying process.

2. The other reason is mathematical probability. Back testing shows that lower-priced stocks appreciate at a faster rate than higher-priced stocks. Using this rule in our selection method, we are adding a momentum rule to the system and buying stocks that have a greater chance of appreciating quickly – maximising the use of our capital.

SELL RULES OF THE I-WANT-MONEY SYSTEM

The stock is sold if the price falls to a trailing stop of 2.5 of its average true range (ATR). The ATR is calculated over a 20-day period.

ATR is a way of measuring the stock's price volatility. In this case, the volatility of the stock over the previous 20 days is calculated, then multiplied by 2.5, providing the trailing sell-stop level.

This method of using a trailing ATR sell-stop level assists the trader by having an order in the market that is active at all times – called a *conditional sell order*.

A conditional order is a pre-set order. If the nominated sell price is reached, the stock is sold.

RESULTS OVER THESE TWO YEARS (11 MAY 2019 – 11 MAY 2021)

- Win rate: 52.5%.

- Average profit win: 11.1%.

- Average loss: 4.48%.

- Pay-off ratio: 2.7 – so with a 52.5% win rate each trade averages a win 2.7 times what it loses.

- Total number of trades executed: 118.

- Maximum pullback of the systems capital: 8.9%.

- Total return on capital over the trading campaign: 99% – capital has not been compounded or reinvested.

Figure 14.1: I-Want-Money System

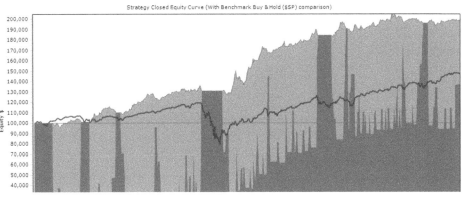

Source: wealth-lab.com

Figure 14.1 displays the rising profit curve.

The dark shaded areas represent capital. This too has a rising profit curve, as profits are banked and not reinvested or compounded.

The single line in the middle of the chart represents an alternative investment, so we can benchmark the systems performance. It shows the result of a buy and hold strategy if one had bought the S&P 500 index. That result was a return of 47.9% compared to the system returning 99%.

It is worth noting that to achieve the buy and hold return of 47.9%, the trader would have been required to hold and not sell the S&P 500 index throughout the significant drawdown in April 2020. This is despite the fact that this benchmark trade was almost 20% below starting capital and 35% below its recent high. This is an important consideration – traders needs to ask themselves if they have the psychological resilience to hold such a trade and not sell during an extremely challenging time.

Alternately, the system exited all positions quickly during the Covid crash as it has done upon other quick market pullbacks. The system is designed to exit quickly, as it doesn't know how steep the falls could be. I will discuss the problem of not knowing in detail in a later chapter: here too, Zen has an answer.

Here are some charts displaying trade examples – to show the system's rules in action.

Figure 14.2: LULU (1)

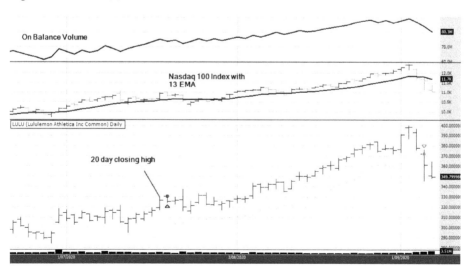

Source: wealth-lab.com

The stock chart of Figure 14.2 shows how the method works. The chart displays three charts in one:

- The top chart is the **On Balance Volume** (OBV).
- The middle chart is the **Nasdaq 100 index** (index symbol NQ).
- The lower chart is the **stock price** action.

Remember that our first rule is to check the Nasdaq 100 and to see whether the closing price is above the 13 EMA before we proceed.

Next, we check whether the stock price has made a 20-day closing high.

Stock price appreciation is also checked. The stock's closing price is to be 8% above the closing price of 20 days ago. If you don't have a computer to do this for you, then a manual countback and calculation will be required.

Next, we want to see volume coming into the stock – so the OBV is to be higher than it was five days ago. Again, a manual countback can be done. However, it's much easier to see by putting the OBV indicator on the chart.

Last (but certainly not least) you can see the dots on the chart – trailing the stock price after entry. As discussed, this is a conditional order placed in the market. If the price falls to that nominated price, the stock is sold at either a profit or a loss. As with most trailing stops, the exit price is never lowered, but stays sideways or is moved up along with the rising price.

The entry price is shown by a dot paired with an upward arrow (as the system purchases rising stocks) and the sell price by a dot paired with a downward arrow (selling as the price falls). The trade displayed in the chart above was a winning trade, resulting in a profit of 12.7%.

However, the two trades displayed on the next chart, following the same buy rules, are both losses. The two entries on the chart both met all the system's rules; then the price fell soon after purchase. The stock price reaches the ATR trailing stop – the safety net signal to sell. This time the strategy is failing, so it sells to preserve capital.

Figure 14.3: LULU (2)

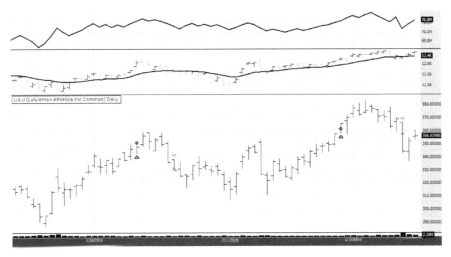

Source: wealth-lab.com

So here you have a method of trading that gives you control.

The system buys stocks that are in strong uptrends; it sells when momentum fades and the stock begins to fall. If the method fails and the stock price falls away before making a profit, the trailing stop (based on a volatility measurement using ATR) takes you out of the trade to preserve capital.

You have a maximum of five trades in the portfolio at a time, sometimes less. Having a maximum of only five open positions at a time makes it an easy portfolio to manage. The number of trades operating in your portfolio will depend on the general market movements at the time. If the index is not trending strongly, you may not have the maximum five trades open.

The system's trades can be made more profitable with advanced position-sizing techniques. I have avoided including those, as beginners' minds may be struggling with too much information. The alternative to advanced position sizing is to simply use larger trade sizes – which is possible on an exchange like the Nasdaq 100, where liquidity is vast.

Some traders may be thinking this system is the best idea since sliced bread and can't wait to get a piece of it. More advanced traders or readers – perhaps those with a background in mathematics or computer science – are thinking, "Let's tweak it for a fatter slice." As we know, it's our thinking that makes the market.

Perhaps now, you are also thinking, "That's better! This is what I want: a technical system that works on clear logic. I knew you were holding back on us. No hocus-pocus Zen reasoning is required!"

I said I would discuss the pros and cons of a method like this. Those considerations are in the next chapter.

Pete's personal trading story

DURING THE YEARS 2012 to 2014, I was living in a monastery studying Buddhism. At the same time, I continued my trading and also taught trading. I approached the monks with the idea that I present a trading course in the lecture hall, donating a generous percentage of the profits to them. They agreed.

To the dismay of my then-business manager, I decided to make the fee for the course *by donation*. He thought I was mad and was concerned I would receive little in payment for my efforts. I disagreed and took the gamble – and his challenge of a bet as to who would be proven right.

"Trading requires decision making," I told the course attendees. "One of your big decisions (and lessons) today is to decide how much the course content and I are worth. Please make your donation and place it at the rear of the room, in a sealed and anonymous envelope."

The amount received was four times my manager's estimate. The monks were grateful; I was chuffed, but my manager was not. His losing bet paid for my helpers on the day.

A ZEN SAYING

Where there is great doubt, there will be great awakening.
Small doubt, small awakening.
No doubt, no awakening.

—

CHAPTER
SUMMARY

- Understanding well the psychology of trading has a lot of merit – it is wise to study it.

- Before choosing a system to trade, consider the motives behind your decisions.

- Before applying a system to the market, understand it extremely well: the devil will always be in the detail.

15

YOUR REQUIRED SCHEDULE TO MAKE MONEY

I *N* any challenging profession, such things as organisation, schedules and routine are important. They reduce the strain on working memory and create structure in an environment that at times may be chaotic. Consider professions that operate regularly in chaotic environments, such as firefighters, ambulance drivers, police officers or soldiers in elite army squadrons. These professions all have structure and systems to implement in times of uncertainty and unpredictability.

The I-Want-Money system in the previous chapter operates on a daily schedule. You will need to have the following skills, equipment, discipline and routine to guarantee you follow the rules and execute trades smoothly:

- A computer with a good back-testing program and trading software programs.

- The ability to program and operate the applicable software.

- Access to a quality data feed.

- Access to reliable internet (with back-up) to operate trading platforms and be able to update data daily.

- Run scans daily on your software program to check for buy and sell signals.

- Adjust the ATR trailing stop daily for each trade you have open.

- Immediately take buy signals when they are generated by the system.

- Monitor closely all sell signals when they are generated by the system.

- Record your trade results in a spreadsheet (or similar) for later revision of the system's performance.

- Record the proficiency of your executions in your trading journal for later revision.

- Create enough time every day before the market opens to run your scans, move stops and place buys or sells.

DISCIPLINE AND KEEPING PEACE OF MIND

You will also need to provide yourself with a quiet place with no distractions, or develop the ability to focus and perform tasks well despite surrounding noise or distraction.

Before starting your computer and opening your programs to work, give yourself time to gather your thoughts and emotions. There will be days when a particular trade looks frightening and you won't feel like buying. There will also be days when the market is buoyant and you won't feel like selling if stock prices are nearing a profit stop. You may say to yourself, "It doesn't make sense," and move your stops – ignoring the rules.

Perhaps you will be tempted to hold on to a falling trade in an attempt to save being stopped, and suffer a loss. You may hope for a rebound, again straying from the rules and using discretionary thinking. Discretionary thinking may be part of the rules of another method. However, if you have committed to a mechanical system, best to stick to it and then review its performance later.

This system on the Nasdaq generates around 60 trades a year, from 252 trading days in the year. You need to be careful you don't miss trades, as the one you miss could be a big winner. If you miss big winners, you destroy the positive expectancy statistics of the system.

You need to be on the ball every day of those 252 days.

MORE OPTIONS

Although it is a profitable system, this system won't make you a lot of money unless you use advanced trade-sizing methods, trade very large position sizes or trade the system on multiple indexes similar in velocity to the Nasdaq.

If you are a full-time trader, it could be a good system to have as an accompaniment to other methods. For example, the system may be included with two other methods to give you three tradeable systems. Those three methods could be using different strategies to take advantage of different market conditions. If you had three systems that each produced 60 trades a year, that would total 180 trades a year (an average of 3.5 trades a week). An amalgamation of strategies would ensure you get regular trading signals. Theoretically, more trades mean more profit, as trade frequency creates more opportunity. Of course, you must have winning systems – and you need to be even more on the ball if you choose to operate multiple systems.

You may be thinking an option would be to automate the system or systems – to make operations more seamless and remove, or at least reduce, emotional challenges. However, you will still need to monitor the systems. I have traded automated systems and they still require monitoring. Sometimes trades are only part-filled, which means you don't get to buy or sell your complete order because of low liquidity at your nominated price. That situation is less common on an index like the Nasdaq, but it does happen. It is more common on less liquid exchanges like the Australian ASX 500.

Brokers' platforms have glitches, and you may get a power blackout. Trading halts of indexes and stocks occur. Daily trading statements from your broker can be incorrect. Sometimes you will have to call your broker to make enquiries and make corrections; the factor of human error cannot be completely removed. If you trade daily systems, you will be checking the market every day, whether the system is automated or not.

You will add more complexity if you are using margin or leverage to fund your portfolio.

You may fancy yourself as a good technical analyst and want to trade in a more discretionary style. Therefore, you could use this daily Nasdaq system and its buy signals as a guide to timing a good entry. You could do the same for the sell signals and use them to short sell. Or you may be a trader using a longer time frame and you could use the buy signals to add to existing positions. In whatever way you choose to trade from the many variables I have mentioned, you will require one very important asset: a calm and peaceful mind.

Now that you have read the bulk of this chapter and the one before it, I will ask you the question I ask at seminars:

Will you consider the merits of Zen trading psychology and thinking, or do you regard it as more beneficial to explore more technical trading methods?

Maybe you want more information, and that's fine – as exploring alternative ideas has a lot of merit.

So here is something else for you to think about – another method to compare to the I-Want-Money System.

In Chapter 2 I discussed a trend-following system – one I never used for the longer term because I thought it was too simple and boring. Figure 15.1 shows the result of a system also used on the Nasdaq 100. It is similar to the I-Want-Money System, yet simpler. It operates on a monthly scale. Yes – monthly. That means all analysis is done on the last trading day of the month, in preparation for the next month's first trading day.

Figure 15.1: Zen Monthly System

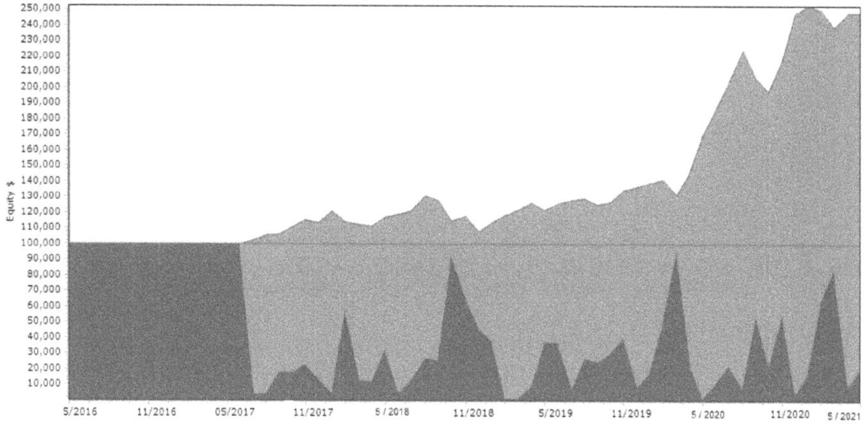

Source: wealth-lab.com

THE RULES OF THE ZEN MONTHLY SYSTEM

- Buy a stock when the closing price is the highest in 12 months.

- Always buy the lowest-priced stock if there is more than one buy signal.

- If you have enough money to buy two stocks, buy the cheapest first then buy the next lowest-price stock.

- Use a trailing stop of 1.5 ATR calculated over two months. Use pre-set market sell orders.

- Use 8% of total equity per trade – which will give you 12 stocks in your portfolio. Compound profits. Keep all trading capital including profits reinvested in the system.

You may notice some similarities with the I-Want-Money System.

Figure 15.2: LULU (3)

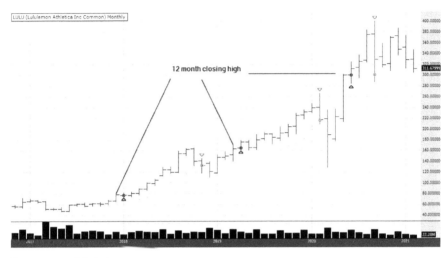

Source: wealth-lab.com

Again using the chart of the stock LULU, we can see how the buying and selling work. The buy signal represents the first trading day of the month. That is the day the system buys, after the stock price makes the highest close in 12 months.

As in the previous system discussed, we use a trailing stop with a sell order placed in the market. This time the setting is 1.5 ATR calculated over a two-month time frame. You can see where the stock is sold when it hits the trailing ATR (the system will re-enter after the next 12-month closing high). The trailing stop exit could happen towards the beginning, middle or end of the month. We don't know. We do know we have a stop in the market.

RESULTS

- The chart above has three trades: the first returning 72%, the second 31% and the third being break-even.

- In four years (17 May to 21 May) the system made 88 trades – 22 trades a year, or a little less than two a month.

- The system had a 60% win rate and averaged a return of 29% a year, turning $100,000 into $248,000.

Systems like this are the ultimate in simplicity for trend following. So simple in methodology. The winning probability of buying trending stocks with price momentum (lowest price) does the heavy lifting for you.

However, you will need to get out of the way, take your hands off the wheel and your finger off the trigger. Trust the process. Trust is level 250 on Dr Hawkins's consciousness scale.

With calmness and peace of mind, less can be more.

YOUR REQUIRED SCHEDULE

This is the same as for the I-Want-Money System, but once a month. Not every trading day.

I can almost hear the protests and questions: "We can't predict markets or cycles."

"What if things had turned out different?"

"We don't know what will happen or whether markets will go up or down."

Zen has an answer to *don't know* and it is in the next chapter.

Pete's personal trading story

In 2013 my trading friend Max and I were working together on mean reversion (MR) systems.[5] Max was the master of MR and developed some clever systems to trade the Australian share market. With me persistently nudging him and after some hesitation on his part, he kindly gave me a system to trade. However, he had a concern. I was predominately a trend trader and I would struggle psychologically with the change of concept. I dismissed his concerns (note: identity/ego/self as a pro trader being challenged).

"I already have enough in my life," he said. Apart from having a partner and family, I was renovating a house, operating trend trading systems, teaching trading, monitoring trades, writing and updating my website along with volunteering at the Buddhist centre. MR systems would require me to short sell and dip buy – something I wasn't used to, not to mention the required monitoring of the semi-automated system (semi-automated because we chose to enter new orders and adjust our existing 100 or so orders manually every morning before the market opened). I managed the system for a few months, during which I became stressed and bug-eyed from so much screen-watching. With my mind now foggy (but being experienced enough to know that was a warning sign), I offered the victory to the market and sold out the system at a loss. Ego grinned, Pete sulked and Max knew it was necessary to say nothing.

---

[5] Mean reversion (MR) systems buy extreme price lows, which are then sold for profit when the stock price returns to its mean average. The method can also short sell highs to be bought back at profit, when the stock price again returns to its mean average. Most MR systems have a very high win rate but a small profit pay-off ratio, so MR systems need to do many trades to be profitable overall and can require intensive monitoring.

A ZEN SAYING

The real cycle you're working on is a cycle called yourself.
Robert M. Pirsig, *Zen and the Art of Motorcycle Maintenance*

(William Morrow and Company, 1974)

—

CHAPTER SUMMARY

- Whatever system or method you choose to trade, psychology (and particularly Zen-think) is a major factor.

- Calmness and peace of mind will greatly assist you – whatever your chosen trading method.

16

ZEN HAS THE ANSWER TO *DON'T KNOW*

*I*f only I knew with certainty what was going to happen. I have pondered that statement many times. Considering that I cannot predict the future, how do I at least try to predict a probable outcome? Surely, there is a way or there is someone or something that can tell me. Unlike many religions, philosophies, economists, trading and investment experts, mathematicians, physicists or proponents of any other field of expertise you can think of, Zen will give you what can seem like a cruel answer: *don't know.*

In April 2015, I wrote a newsletter to my subscribers titled *What if.* I will remind readers who may not recall that negativity and fear about the stock market were extremely prevalent in 2015. There was no recognition of the six-year bull market since the GFC lows of 2009. Fear and caution were the talk of the times. We now know that the five years between early 2015 and 2020 were very strong, and the narrative in early 2020 became, "We have been in a bull market for ten years!" But the view in 2015 was that the markets were still in a six-year recovery mode from the GFC.

Market commentators of the present have short memories about the past, forgetting or dismissing what the emotions of market participants were during different time periods. It appears to be human nature to focus on the negative and it seems many are subconsciously programmed to be cautious and fearful.

Below is what I wrote in 2015 to address the fears of my clients. The newsletter is still on my website.

"WHAT IF"

"What if" is a question I hear from many investors and traders.

- What if interest rates rise?
- What if the housing market collapses?
- What if the stock market collapses?
- What if global stimulus doesn't work?
- What if the global debt sends the world economies into another great depression?
- What if we have hyperinflation and money becomes almost worthless?
- What if we have deflation and assets become almost worthless?
- What if there is a war?
- What if Europe falls into total chaos via a collapse of the euro?
- What if the Chinese economy collapses?
- What if it's all just a global bubble and a house of cards destined to end in certain disaster?

Some or all of the above could be valid concerns. Which "what if" should we worry about the most? Which ones are more likely and in what order will the above scenarios unfold? How safe will we be and how do I support my family and friends? The safest thing to do is probably nothing, it's all too uncertain and dangerous.

Investing and particularly trading is for mugs!

ASK NOT WHY, BUT WHAT

When I was living in a monastery, one of the most thought-provoking and wisest statements I heard was "Ask not why, but what." The philosophy is this: if you continually ask why something has happened or is happening (particularly to yourself), it sends you down the path of wanting and needing to know the reason behind everything that has, or will happen.

To ask what is happening will give you a clearer answer and puts your mind in a place to respond accordingly, instead of worrying incessantly about needing to know why. Is it really necessary to know why a trade is moving in or out of favour? You could ask **what is** happening and then respond. If it is rising, buy. If it is falling, sell. The reasons **why** are nearly always given after the fact.

AN ALTERNATIVE VIEW TO "WHAT IF"

- What if interest rates stay low for many years?

- What if the housing market does not collapse but slows to a steady long-term growth?

- What if the stock market does not collapse?

- What if global stimulus does work?

- What if the global debt slowly erodes via steady growth and a rebuild of confidence?

- What if we have moderate inflation stimulating healthy asset growth?

- What if we have deflation in areas that assist the economy e.g., energy costs continue to decrease stimulating households and business?

- What if there is no war?

- What if Europe does not fall into chaos and slowly rebuilds?

- What if China and India pick up the European slack and drive the world economies?

- What if we are on the verge of an incredible period of prosperity like never witnessed before, driven by technology, emerging economies, and competitiveness.

Some or all could be a pipe dream, some a reality. Which "what if" should we focus our energy on and invest in? What ones are more likely and in what order will the above scenarios unfold? The best thing to do is sell the farm, borrow against the home, leverage ourselves to the eyeballs and invest in anything that moves!

I trade and teach mostly trend trading. It is called trend trading because the methodology focuses on investing in assets that are rising then using risk control in case it does not perform. Not performing does not mean that you got it wrong. It is just that the particular scenario did not work out the way we had hoped.

Absolutely nobody knows what will happen. The above "what ifs" are **impossible** to ascertain to any extent or in what order those things may happen.

THE COVID CRISIS OF 2020 PROVES WE DON'T KNOW

As I write, the world is attempting to recover from the Covid crisis. With the benefit of hindsight, we know that less than half of the negatives listed in my April 2015 newsletter ever happened. Interestingly, more than half of the positives I mentioned have happened. Property markets have not crashed and stock markets have recovered quickly. Interest rates have stayed low. Despite unexpected events such as Brexit and the election of Donald Trump as president of the United States, the global economy and the economies of many individual countries have thrived in the five years between 2015 and 2020. Markets have risen and profits have been made.

It's fair to say that five years ago no one would have been able to predict how things would be today – particularly that the world would suffer from a pandemic and the lives and fortunes of so many would be affected in such dramatic ways. Nor could they know that markets would rebound so quickly from the Covid-induced sell off. Attempting to predict the future of markets now is as pointless as it was then. So rather than worrying, wondering and regretting lost opportunity from inaction caused by fear, you could contemplate a new approach.

That approach is the Zen philosophy of *don't know*.

I said at the start of this book that traders have a great fear of the outcome. If only we knew the outcome of our decisions, trading and life would all be so easy. We want to know, we may think we know, or perhaps we feel we are supposed to know. In our society there is incredible bias towards having to know and find solutions to reduce uncertainty. I suggest this mindset produces a world of people living with constant anxiety. Then we are presented with an appeal from Zen teachers, also from experienced traders, to consider something radical: admit the truth that we don't know and see what happens. If we wholeheartedly accept that appeal, it can change everything.

Don't know doesn't mean *stupid*. It means what I said in the newsletter: to ask *what* is happening, rather than the less useful question of *why*. The question "Why is it happening?" gets you stuck in the desire to know all the answers. The more astute question, "What is happening?" gives you a definitive answer which will lead you on to a corresponding course of action. If what is happening is that the market is falling and giving you sell signals, sell. If what is happening is that the market is rising and giving you buy signals, buy. Your actions may be to sell, buy, hold or stand aside and wait. Those four actions are valid responses to the question of "What is happening?" During the extremely fast sell-off in March 2020, no one really knew all the *whys* and *what ifs*, but we all certainly knew what was happening – the market was falling fast! If you had a definitive plan for your trading, the appropriate action was to respond to what was *happening* – the answer to why it was happening would surely come in time.

The Zen teacher Suzuki Roshi once said, "A beginner's mind is wide open and questioning. An expert's mind is closed."

So, the statement, "Don't know" actually gives us flexibility of mind. The alternatives of "I know" or "I need to know" can eliminate fluid thinking and render us rigid from our own mental and cultural conditioning. We often fill our minds with assumptions in our constant grasping at *knowing*. This is a state of mind that can freeze with inaction. Not having to know is what creates the flexibility of mind that is needed to be a master trader. In our lives it often seems there is immense competition between those who think they know the most – but do those who know a lot always produce good trading results? If this were true, all the very intelligent people that exist would be successful trading geniuses – we know this is not the case.

WHAT WE DO KNOW

We know that people who do not plan, and therefore make unmeasured decisions, often fail. People who do plan and make measured decisions, based on probability and risk control, often succeed. We also know that those who trust and release themselves into a process (level 250 on Dr Hawkins's consciousness scale) have a better chance of producing a positive result. Importantly, they also have a process to measure results and change if required.

If we met and discussed the dynamic results from systems in this book, you might exclaim, "Yes, but it has been a bull market!"

And I would reply to you, "I didn't know it would be."

What if you then asked, "Is it a good time to start the system now?"

And I replied, "I don't know."

And then you thought, "Well, what sort of a trading coach is he? He doesn't know!"

Trading is about probability and doing the best we can in an uncertain environment. It is not about knowing what is going to happen, because you should realise by now – no one knows.

The proficient trader knows that anything can happen in the market: stocks can fall quickly and stocks can rally to incredible values. That is why the trader must be ready to respond and not react – to many possibilities.

When we buy an uptrending stock, we do not know whether it will be a losing trade or a winning trade. We do not know how much it will lose or how much it will win. What we do have is the probability of our method. For example, using a probable method of trend trading shows us that if we follow the process of selling downtrending stocks and buying and holding uptrending stocks, we have a good chance of success. The market is unpredictable because we don't know how market participants will react.

The market is a mass of human emotion and, as any behavioural economist, professional trader or Zen teacher will tell you, attempting to predict what that mass of minds will do is impossible.

A ZEN STORY

A student went to the master and asked, "What happens after death?"

"I don't know," came the reply.

"Are you not a Zen master?" asked the student. "Why don't you know?"

"I am not dead yet," said the master.

—

A Taishin Shodo story

WHEN I WAS on retreat in Japan, one of my fellow participants was an ex-soldier who had experienced three tours of duty in Iraq and Afghanistan. He was struggling with retreat life, announcing one day during a meal with the head Zen priest present that he needed sex, something to drink and different food. He would go to a bar in a seaside port a few hours away, satisfy his desires and then return in a few days to continue the retreat. The elderly priest looked at him and just said, "Okay." I was astonished, for I was a regular retreat attendee and had never experienced anything like this.

The next day the head priest and I delivered the ex-soldier to the closest railway station. On the way back to the Zen temple, I expressed my opinion: he would not be back; he was disrespectful, undisciplined; he would be unable to tear himself away from his addictions; he probably had PTSD. I had him judged, labelled and thought I knew it all. The priest said nothing, just nodded.

A few days later, the ex-soldier returned at the time and day he said he would. Settling back into retreat life, he commented on how he had missed the routine, structure and serenity. He then became one of the most dedicated meditators I have ever had the honour to sit with. The head priest never said anything. He didn't need to. The ex-soldier and I had both learned our lesson. You just don't know.

CHAPTER SUMMARY

- When analysing the market, ask "What is happening?" not so much "Why is it happening?"

- I don't know what will happen. Nor do you, or anyone.

- Embrace the fact you don't know. It will free your mind of worry and the need to over-analyse everything.

- We do know over-analysis can create stagnation, not the fluidity of thinking and action the trader needs.

17

SIMPLE PRACTICES FOR COMPLICATED PROCESSES

I BELIEVE trading can be easy, but we make it hard. It is not our fault that we make it hard; it is because we have not learned the correct way of thinking to make it easier. That way of thinking has been described in detail in the previous chapters. However, despite how well we may develop our minds to cope with what trading and life present to us, there is no escaping the need for practical solutions. From my own trading experience, as well as my observation of clients and students, I have listed what I regard as the greatest challenges for those of us who choose to make trading a part of our lives.

WHEN TO START

When to start trading is a common question. The reason people put off starting to trade is fear. Often, the fear is because the market is high and they are afraid that it has had its run; that it will start to fall. When the market is low, people are afraid because they are influenced by the negativity all around them. It is impossible to know when is a good time or when is a bad time. The answer to "When?" is probably "Now." There is an old Chinese saying: "The best time to plant a tree is 20 years ago."

WHAT TO TRADE

Many traders experiment with diverse trading vehicles. By *vehicle,* I mean ways to trade, such as using shares, options, warrants, exchange traded funds, contracts for difference, commodities, cryptocurrencies, foreign exchange – the list is vast. If you are struggling to make a profit from trading, you need to simplify your process and work more on your mind. The best way to simplify is to avoid the exotic and complicated trading vehicles that exist. I simplify my process by trading shares in my own country's currency and using my country's stock exchange, the Australian Stock Exchange. Because of that choice, I do business with institutions in my own area and trade during my local business hours. I do these things to normalise my life as much as possible. I regard trading in a foreign currency (using foreign institutions) and having to work during inconvenient hours as complicated and tiring. The choice is yours, however my experience is that many traders attempt too many ideas and diversification, resulting in emotional and physical burnout. You may have no choice but to trade overseas, but for practical and lifestyle reasons, explore your own exchanges first and look at ways to simplify your process.

WHAT TIME FRAME TO TRADE

As mentioned in Chapter 3, arguably one of the hardest decisions to make when looking to choose or develop a system to trade is what time frame you will use.

Considering that statistically 90–95% of traders lose or break even, it seems logical that *increasing* your trading time frame to weekly charts for analysis is the best option to put you in an area where the winners exist and away from the anxiety-ridden losers poring over charts every day.

If you are a beginner, then you are best to avoid short-term trading. Most traders over-trade and most traders lose. Therefore, why join the losing team? To maintain calmness and peace of mind, you need a time frame that is short enough to provide the number of trades required to keep you interested, but long enough to give you time to think, detach, respond but not react. Many traders find using a weekly time frame to be ideal – particularly if they have other responsibilities such as work or family.

DRAWDOWN

Portfolio drawdown, which means a pullback in your equity, is by far one of the most difficult challenges most traders face. In fact, I would say it is *the* most difficult challenge. The size of your drawdown will depend on the method you trade. If you are a short-term trader, exits are normally *tight* (this means intended exits are set close to the prevailing price, so if the trade moves opposite to your expectation, losses are kept small). However, this means you will most probably be doing frequent trades as the system will sell and buy often, because of its tight parameters.

If you are using a trend trading method like some of the systems discussed in this book, exits are normally looser and set further away from the prevailing price. Therefore, swings in equity value are inevitable.

Many traders struggle with finding the balance between frequency of trades and portfolio drawdown.

They are attracted to the minimal trading and large profits that trend trading systems can deliver, but dislike the inevitable drawdowns that these systems also produce. Drawdown is the destroyer of many trading careers. Traders sell their portfolio at the worst possible time and then see it recover substantially.

HOW MUCH CAPITAL TO START WITH

Considering drawdown is perhaps the biggest challenge for traders, the following is what I advise clients: think of an amount of money that you can afford to lose. An amount that will not affect your life in an adverse way. For example, in the event of an equity pullback of your nominated amount, you would be able to pay the rent or mortgage, pay bills, feed the family, not create strained relations with your partner and still sleep soundly at night? What dollar figure is tolerable to you? If you said that amount is $15,000 and you are trading a system with a 15% historical drawdown, then your starting capital would be no more than $100,000 – as 15% of $100,000 is $15,000: the amount you nominated as tolerable. Of course, to do the above calculation, you need to know your trading method's historical drawdown.

Your tolerable figure needs to be an amount that, during market volatility, you will not panic and sell (disobeying your rules). All systems experience equity pullback. You need to be able to emotionally withstand a pullback should one or both of the following things happen:

1. The portfolio equity has a pullback and you are able to stick to the system rules – capital value recovers and starts to rise again.

2. All your trades are sold out from your stop loss rules and your portfolio is converted to cash – this may happen during volatile market corrections.

You now have a worst-case scenario: a loss of $15,000. If that is too much for you, then you can halve your portfolio capital to $50,000, reducing your worse-case scenario to a loss of $7,500 – because that is 15% of $50,000. If you can withstand a larger worst-case dollar figure, then raise (or lower) the portfolio size to your emotional tolerance level.

Alternatively, trade a method with a lower historical drawdown. However, trading is a game of give and take. As mentioned, implementing a system with a lower drawdown will mean having tighter stops, resulting in more trades. You will need to find your personal compromise between how many trades your system does and how much you are prepared to let the equity swing up and down.

BUYING AND SELLING

Some traders struggle to buy and others find it easy. I have noticed two dominant personality traits among clients. Those who are confident and often successful in other areas of life apart from trading have no problem committing and buying. They have been right in their experience of other ventures, so in their mind there is nothing to fear about trading. However, they have problems in selling, often because they do not have a pre-determined exit. They are confident people and feel they don't need one, because they rarely envision failure or losing. At times, they won't sell because that means they are wrong and defeated! Loss is a rare occurrence for these successful and positive-thinking people.

The other personality trait I have noticed in traders is in those who struggle to buy. These are the conservative and often analytical types with an aversion to risk. They finally muster the courage to buy, normally accompanied by reluctance and trepidation. Because of their excellent analytical skills and research, they often choose trades with a good probability of success. However, their worry and fear consume them, and they find it hard to hold trades. They tend to sell at the first sign of a pullback. They pre-empt sell signals and don't wait for sell confirmation from their rules. They place sell orders too close to the prevailing stock price and become victims of whips in volatility from the market, selling unnecessarily. After being stopped out prematurely, they later see their trades continue in the direction they first anticipated. If they get a sell signal, they are often disciplined and sell ASAP, so they never lose much. Unfortunately, they don't win much either because they find it difficult to hold trends, often selling before the trade has run to fruition and returned a handsome profit.

The practical answer to both of these personality traits (along with Zen-think), and many other fear-based errors while trading, is good position sizing. Position sizing means determining the dollar size of a trade to suit your risk tolerance. Position sizing and exits are far more important factors in your trading than entries. It can take many years for the beginner to realise this, which results in losses and lost opportunity. Do not be one of those traders – put the effort into learning about safe and profitable ways to size your trades.

STICKING TO A PROCESS

This whole book is written to explain why traders cannot stick to a process. Sticking to a process is the most valuable thing you will ever do to improve your trading. Selecting or developing a method and committing to it for a period of time will do more for your technical and psychological development than anything else.

For example, if you are using a weekly trend trading system similar to the one described in this book, I suggest a 12-month period of commitment to experience and learn about the market, your method and your mind. Using a shorter-term system, you could reduce that to a one- to three-month time frame.

No book, course, seminar, coach, mentor, YouTube video or anything else will teach you more about trading than if you do it, stick to it and record it with your own blood, sweat and tears. Good training and coaching are essential, but they are useless without you committing to a process.

HOW TO LEARN TRADING

The master appears when the student is ready.

I really believe the saying above. Most aspiring traders are very reluctant to pay for tuition – some with good reason. There are many incompetent and overly expensive teachers in this profession. Many aspiring traders never pay for anything. They scour the internet looking for the cheapest option. They can become victim to unscrupulous salespeople who make unfounded promises of quick or eternal riches. If you are serious about being a successful trader, then get some quality tuition. When searching for a teacher, use your common sense. Join a trading group or club and ask others about their experiences. Google some reviews, email or ring the teacher and ask to speak to their past clients. And, last but not least, see whether the teacher discloses their trading results. This is a real indication of the experience and confidence of the teacher. However, keep in mind that to be a great coach, you don't always have to be the best player, trader or even Zen practitioner.

WHEN TO STOP

If you are constantly losing or have not been regularly profitable for some time, you should stop trading now.

This is a logical and simple remedy to the problem, but it can be very difficult emotionally. If you are losing or unprofitable and cannot stop, I suggest you are addicted to trading. The reason for your losses or lack of performance is likely to be deeply psychological. It is unlikely to be a technical issue. The problem may not be your method or the market, but your mind. If you think that is a harsh statement, consider Albert Einstein's famous saying, "The definition of insanity is to repeat the same process and expect a different outcome."

This is a serious problem and a huge impediment to your trading goals and aspirations. It is also a very common issue. So, if what I am writing resonates with you, please do not feel incompetent. You are one of many struggling with the same issue. I have said many times, trading is simple technically but difficult emotionally. Your emotional understanding and resilience need to be raised to a level that can cope with the method you are using. Or you may need to lower the complexity of your method to suit your level of emotional competence. You are at a stage in your trading where some deep soul-searching needs to be done and hopefully the next chapter will help with that process.

A ZEN SAYING

"If you understand real practice, then archery or any other activity can be Zen. If you don't understand how to practice archery in its true sense, then even though you practice very hard, what you acquire is **just** technique. It won't help you through and through. Perhaps you can hit the mark without trying, but without that bow and arrow, you cannot do anything. If you understand the point of practice, then even without a bow and arrow, the archery will help you. How you get that kind of power or ability, is only through right practice."

Shunryu Suzuki

Pete's personal story

I REGARD MY personality type as one that fits the slightly anxious, analytical trader. A trader who is good at taking stops, can baulk at buy signals and sometimes likes to be out of the market to take a mental and emotional break. In early 2017, I travelled to Japan to further my studies in Zen. My portfolio had been in a lengthy sideways trend. I reasoned it was a good time to take a break and focus on Zen study, so I liquidated my portfolio. The planned spiritual sabbatical was challenging and tiring. My difficult feelings were compounded by the news of a young and close family member being killed in an accident. Being away in a remote location, I was unable to attend the funeral back home in Australia. My resilience was being challenged.

On my return home, the markets had changed and rallied. My system was signalling a re-entry into the market immediately. The last thing I felt like doing was buying. I had expected (and would have liked) a longer break. I knew that, like Zen, trading is a process – and the process was asking me to commit once again. With reluctance and gritted teeth, I bought back in. Two years later that system was up 72%.

Trading can be easy, but we make it hard.

CHAPTER SUMMARY

- Most traders tend to make trading complicated.

- After some rigorous study, start as soon as you can – it is wise to start with a small account.

- Trade on your local exchange in your own country's currency – it is usually easier.

- Choose a trading time frame that does not make you feel overwhelmed.

- Less starting capital will reduce the uncomfortable experience of a big drawdown.

- Size your trades to minimise risk.

- Pick a process, stick to it, then test and measure its performance.

- If you are not making progress, stop and evaluate your method and mindset.

18

THE FINAL WORD
ON MASTERY

MASTER THAT MEDITATION

*I*N the first chapter, I discussed mathematical edges. However, there is another edge in trading that is rarely discussed: the Zen edge gained from meditation.

Trading is taught in many ways and there are different techniques. Meditation also has many variations of technique. In Western culture, two techniques are commonly practised:

1. The *concentration method*, assisted by visualisation, to help focus the mind.

2. The *insight method*, to attain awareness of thoughts.

Some examples of visualisation methods are: verbally-guided meditations asking you to imagine pleasant scenes (this practice may often be accompanied by soft music in the background); focusing on one thought or object, such as reciting a mantra or concentrating on the heart; or using an anecdotal method, in which the meditator attempts to consciously reverse thoughts of hate or anger – transforming them into love and compassion.

The insight technique encourages you to lay down the mind's tools of thinking and analysis, so as to gain insight into what is guiding your perceptions. This is more like the Zen method. An example of the insight technique used by Zen practitioners is the simple process of observing only the breath. This allows the body and mind to settle, and then detach naturally, without the help of visualisations or a particular concentration method. The Zen method is not guided with music or verbal prompts, except for beginner practitioners. The Zen/insight method of meditation can be more difficult to master, but is in my opinion more beneficial. For it is the introspection of our thinking that leads to greater awareness.

To trade well, you need to be very aware of how you are thinking.

It is normal for our minds' thoughts to wander; one of the main aims of insight meditation is to teach the mind to wander a little less (hopefully a lot less). Then it can perceive with more clarity.

The key to Zen meditation is the ability to perceive clearly without the distraction of judging and labelling thought.

The doors to destructive judging and distraction need to be closed. If you can close those doors, then another will open: the door to perception and clarity. With that clarity, peace of mind naturally occurs, accompanied by the benefits of insight and awareness. This is how the *letting go* process works: let go of your judgements to allow a new paradigm of thinking to enter. However, there is one common challenge for all of us that seek clarity of thought: understanding our past conditioning.

Our personalities are formed from a combination of nature (our individual biology) and nurture (societal and family influences). Zen philosophy believes all humans seek security and identity. Our minds quickly attach to what we have been encouraged to learn and what we know. We then form beliefs in our mind about what we think we know.

We are all conditioned, or *programmed*, from an early age; this is normal for every culture. Many people live their lives without ever questioning, or developing an inquiring mind. They never awaken to the fact that their minds have been conditioned to think a certain way. The terms *awakening* and *enlightenment* are simply descriptions of an evolved way of thinking beyond the norm. Skilful traders become aware of their thinking and learn to respond calmly to any situation in the present, rather than react with a conditioned mind living with past trauma or an anxious mind living in the future. This has been discussed at length in previous chapters, but what follows is a summary of the process of thinking that you need to develop to trade like a Zen master.

THE ORDER OF MASTERY

1. BECOME AWARE OF YOUR THINKING VIA MEDITATION

I have already discussed meditation and the benefits of the practice. You will recall that meditation is the sixth rule of the *peace and profit* system discussed in Chapter 10. Before you begin to recognise that you habitually judge and label everything you think, you first need to be aware of just your thoughts. You will learn this skill if you use insight meditation regularly.

2. DO NOT JUDGE OR LABEL YOUR THOUGHTS

I discussed this in detail in Chapter 6. You will also learn this skill if you meditate regularly. The objective is to train the mind to observe its thoughts rather than let it move immediately to needing to solve or fix. Observe the mind's tendency to judge and label thoughts and what it thinks is wrong – or right!

3. RECOGNISE YOUR ATTACHMENTS

We explored attachment and its importance in Chapter 4. Very few people realise how their minds attach very quickly to one perspective – rarely considering that there are other possibilities or opportunities. Master your attachments and you will master your mind. Master your mind and you will begin to see and experience a different market. This is when it is beneficial to remember the Buddha's second Noble Truth from Chapter 3: "The cause of suffering is attachment."

4. STICK TO A SIMPLE TRADING METHOD FOR A PERIOD

This is similar to the advice given to aspiring Zen practitioners, which is: stick to the Five Precepts (discussed in Chapter 9) and meditate often. One of the best ways to improve as a trader is to stick to a simple method, then work on your mind. You will realise by now that the greatest challenge is your mind and the way it thinks about trading. Devote yourself to that challenge and you will reap the rewards. If you are struggling to stick to your method, then either your method does not suit your personality or your mind needs to be trained to see things from a Zen perspective. Or perhaps the problem is a combination of both.

5. SIZE, BUY, SELL, REPEAT

Trading is a process. There are only four things you need to do repetitively to complete that process: size your trade, put your trade on, take your trade off, and repeat the process.

In Australia, we have a gambling game called *two-up*. Two people flip a coin up in the air and bet on whether the coin will land on the ground heads-up or heads-down. There is a 50% chance of winning with each toss of the coin because the head is only on one side. If you bet $1 you have a 50% chance of winning a dollar or losing a dollar. Now, if you have a trading method that has a 50% win rate and that returns $2.30 each time you win and loses $1 each time you lose, is it a winning system? Yes, clearly it is (note that $2.30 or 2.3 to 1 was the payoff ratio of the I-Want-Money System). So why would you not keep flipping that coin? In this case the coin represents the trading system. If you have a trading method based on a similar winning probability, just keep sizing, buying, selling and repeating. If you do not know your method's probability, you are indulging in the first of the two reasons for trading failure that were discussed in Chapter 1:

1. You don't have a system or method to trade (because of a lack of knowledge).

2. Even if you do have a method, you don't stick to it (because you have not developed a Zen state of mind).

At the beginning of this book, I said my objective was to connect the philosophies and techniques of trading with Zen. It was also to show readers the value of embracing Zen into their trading and lives – to improve not only their financial situation, but their happiness and overall well-being. I want to give you an example of someone who has done that in another career, and I will let that person say it in his own words. Those words were spoken in an interview with this famous person and posted on the blog *Amuse* in April 2018.

MEDITATION

I do meditation and yoga out of a need to have an optimal state of mind and peace and calm, and at the same time happiness and joy. Everybody has their ways to reach that state of consciousness where you're in a good mood and you feel love towards yourself, towards people around you, towards the planet. So, I try to be aligned with this kind of approach and mindset in life. It was definitely not an easy period for me in the last 7–8 months. The

---

results were not there in the big tournaments. But more than results, it was that lack of balance emotionally.

LIFESTYLE

My gluten intolerance was discovered in 2010. Before that I didn't even know what gluten was. I also removed the dairy products and refined sugar from my diet as well, which is maybe even more important than gluten. I think that has helped me not only to be a better tennis player throughout my career in the last seven years but also a healthier person, an athlete that recovers faster. It worked for me, obviously. I'm not saying this is the way to go for everyone. But it's something that has been a very important, integral part of my career, of my life.

FEARS

I work very hard every single day to not have any fears. I think that fears are the biggest enemy of all of us in every aspect of our beings, whatever we do. If I paid too much attention to my fears, I wouldn't be able to achieve what I have.

LOVE AND CONSCIOUSNESS

I try to focus on the positive emotions that drive me, like passion, joy and the pure inspiration to play the sport that I love. I have to always go back to that core: the fact that I enjoy just holding a racket and playing on a daily basis on any regular court, not just the centre court of Grand Slams, brings me that excitement and that joy that pushes me to keep on going. So, I've had to rediscover this inner joy of motivation, of playing. And not only to win or lose, but playing for the sake of enjoying the game.

Personally, my life as a tennis player has changed since then. Not in a way of not having enough motivation or playing enough tournaments, but entering a new dimension of consciousness and being aware of myself as more than just a tennis player. Now when I come home I have to leave the racket on the side and commit to the family duties, which I enjoy very much. And I think that brings me that sense of calmness and great recovery as well.

If you have not yet realised who this man is, he is the tennis legend Novak Djokovic. As I write in 2021, he has just won another Australian Open: his eighth. Presently, this is the highest number of Australian Opens won by any player. That particular contest was arguably one of his hardest ever – sports commentators unanimously agreed it was his mental edge that won him the tournament. Novak eloquently describes the qualities he has found important to his professional and personal success. He has also unknowingly summarised the philosophies and techniques in this book – with the same precision he displays in his profession.

Without exactly saying it, Novak understands the importance of detaching from outcomes while still having incredible commitment to success. He has realised detachment comes more easily if he places less importance on himself and his ego. He has also learned to commit to a healthy lifestyle, meditate and once again find the joy and excitement in his game (unfortunately, this is something that many traders lose because of stress). Remember how excited you were when you first discovered trading? Or perhaps you are new to trading and can't wait to get started. Too many let that excitement morph into obsession and fear, destroying not only their joy of trading, but their joy of life.

The Zen trader learns to be humble and let go of wanting so many things their way. *Your way* is only your current perception; it may not be the best way for you – or for others.

RETREAT, AS A GOOD WARRIOR SOMETIMES DOES, TO FIGHT ANOTHER DAY

If you are ever brave enough to attend a meditation retreat, the following is what will happen: the many things we regularly use to distract our minds will be removed from your presence. Television, computers, mobile phones, reading material, radio, music – even talking is sometimes banned, as many retreats have periods of silence. Beginners sometimes find the thought of a silent retreat a little daunting, not to say frightening. However, most participants go on to find the experience of silence one of the most beneficial and joyful of the retreat.

Your food intake is purified as much as possible by the serving of healthy and mostly vegetarian food. There is no alcohol, no coffee (tea is sometimes allowed), and other drinks of a stimulant nature are restricted or discouraged. In most cases, gentle exercise like yoga or walking is encouraged.

The focus of the retreat is, of course, on meditation.

The restrictions imposed upon you are not sadistic measures to drive you crazy through deprivation. The purpose is for you to realise how much your daily habits and mild addictions distract you from gaining awareness. The thoughtful reader may have realised what the well-meaning intent of the retreat planner is: to make it easy for you to stick to the Five Precepts, so all you have to focus on is your meditation.

Retreats remove the pressure and temptation present in everyday life, making it easier to stick to the first five rules of the system. This largely frees you of responsibility and allows you to focus on introspection. In the way a good trading coach can elevate your understanding and ability to trade, a well-organised retreat can elevate your level of consciousness. A higher level of consciousness will raise your level of calm and presence, therefore improving your ability to trade well. As I said earlier, incorporating trading and Zen is not some genius mathematical trading system combined with secret powers, handed down from an ageing master living on a mountaintop. It is a simple system of living a wholesome life to the best of your ability and combining it with meditation.

Good traders adopt simple systems; simplicity and discipline are the key to success and profits. Zen masters adopt simple systems; simplicity and discipline are the key to calm and presence. So as aspiring traders, we need to be aspiring humans. It's a full circle we need to travel. Always.

FINAL ADVICE

My final advice to you on your journey of trading and life mastery is this: do your best to regularly include the six rules of the Buddha's system in your life. These are the Five Precepts and meditation. When you lose discipline or make errors, it is all part of the path, and no one is perfect. I have fallen from the way many times. Take a breath and come back to the system that develops calmness and peace of mind. Those are the most important qualities to have for a happy and contented life, and to trade well.

Trading can be a repetitive process; so is Zen. With that in mind and to finish this book, I will repeat what I said at the start.

The similarities between trading and Zen are immense. Both are simple processes, but not necessarily easy to follow. The rewards are also immense, both personally and professionally. As traders, we need to look at methods that work, have merit and are proven over time. Zen is such a method.

A ZEN SAYING

Buddhist meditation, but above all that of Zen, seeks not to explain but to pay attention, to become aware, to be mindful, in other words to develop a certain kind of consciousness that is above and beyond deception by verbal formulas – or by emotional excitement.

Thomas Merton

A final story from both Pete and Taishin Shodo

FOR PETE THE trader, 2019 was one of my best years trading and coaching. My portfolio was performing well, I was teaching many clients and travelling often, presenting seminars inter-state. Book sales were good. I was feeling happy and confident.

Also in 2019, my Zen teacher took a much-needed break. Being the next-most experienced practitioner, I accepted the responsibility of filling his shoes to the best of my ability. I became Taishin, the Zen teacher. I enjoyed the role and learned much more than I had anticipated, and my fellow practitioners and newcomers seemed to warm to me. Despite some very challenging personal responsibilities outside of trading and Zen, I was feeling happy and confident.

Early 2020 marked the onset of the Covid pandemic. My system experienced a bigger pullback than my modelling had shown. The speed of the market fall added another layer of intensity. I was surprised at the level of emotion I was feeling. I noticed my mind asking, "I am trained in Zen; why am I suffering so much?" I also noticed my mind challenging its conceived identity of trader, coach, writer and Zen priest.

I was aware of my thoughts and their habitual tendency to judge and label – thoughts like regretting the past and being fearful of the future. My mind also searched for my personal identity: the identity of who or what it liked to think I was. I managed to follow the rules of my method, until more market falls meant my stops being hit and the exiting of all my trades.

I went back to the drawing board.

I reconsidered my methods and formulated others, wrote in my journal, meditated, went to the gym. I spoke to colleagues in trading and Zen. Friends and trusted students, some of whom are now like colleagues, did not escape my need for disclosure and doubt. I listened to podcasts on trading psychology, exposed my thoughts and feelings to my partner and tried very hard not to revenge trade!

In short, I did what is in this book. I practised what I preach. Not perfectly, but to the best of my ability. After all, it was just another lesson along the trading and Zen path. The lessons seem never-ending, but are worth their weight in gold.

Trading and Zen are unique paths to follow. The paths for each of us are as diverse as our minds.

I hope to see many of you on the path with me.

BIBLIOGRAPHY

Rather than list the hundreds of books I have read, the following four are those I regard as being instrumental in my trading and Zen career.

TRADING BOOKS

The New Trading for a Living by Dr Alexander Elder (Wiley, 2014).

Dr Elder's book was the first book that made me realise the importance of psychology in trading. I still recommend this book to my clients, particularly the first third of the book explaining how the trader's mind works.

One Good Trade by Mike Bellafiore (Wiley, 2010).

Mike was one of the first trading teachers I noticed who emphasised focusing intently on one trade at a time, to be with that trade, here and now. We share a love of golf and that sport can be similar to trading. You play best when you focus and hit one ball at a time. Focus on doing that and your golf (and trading) score will look after itself.

ZEN AND BUDDHIST BOOKS

After the Ecstasy the Laundry by Jack Kornfield (Rider, 2000).

So many good Buddhist books and so many esteemed authors: the Dalai Lama, Daniel Goleman, Thich Nhat Hanh, Shunryu Suzuki and Pema Chodron, to name just a few. However, I have a passion for incorporating Zen Buddhism into Western culture and Jack does this so well with his books. As the title suggests, despite our successes in any field, we need to return to the basics and just do the mundane work – be that trading or a form of self-actualisation like Zen.

OTHER RELATED BOOKS

Destructive Emotions: A Scientific Dialogue with the Dalai Lama (Bantam, 2004).

Daniel Goleman's association with the Dalai Lama, merging science and Buddhism, was ground-breaking work. The book explores the thinking of some of the greatest philosophical and scientific minds, bringing Buddhism and neuroscience together. This book opened my eyes to the possibilities that exist – within an open mind!

MORE INFORMATION ABOUT TOPICS IN THIS BOOK

Articles about trading mind-set, meditation, trading courses and systems (including more detail about the systems in this book) are available on my website: www.easysharetradingsystems.com.au.

ACKNOWLEDGEMENTS

Any book, no matter how big or small, requires significant input from others. I am most grateful for the help, advice and patience given by the following people. Sincere thanks to my partner (and clinical psychologist) Cynthia Hip-Waye, for her professional and untiring input. Dr Elder for his help and constructive criticism. The Australian Technical Analysts Association and other trading groups for regularly inviting me to lecture, stimulating my desire to continue research and development. The monks at the Kadampa Meditation Centre (my past home) in Wamberal NSW, for their acceptance, support and meditation training. My Zen teacher in Australia, Jishin Hoka, without whom the Silky Oak Zen group would not exist. All the members of Silky Oak Zen for their love and support. Koro Kaisin (for just being), head teacher at Open Gate Zendo (Boundless Mind Zen school) in Olympia, Washington State, USA. My past students, clients and fellow members of trading brainstorming groups for posing their challenging questions. Last but not least, to all my friends and family who have encouraged me (despite their bewilderment at times) to continue on with my trading, writing and Zen.

DISCLAIMER

The material presented in this book neither professes to be, nor is intended to be, advice to trade or to invest in any specific financial instrument or to use any particular methods of trading or investing. Readers should not act on the basis of any information without properly considering its applicability to their financial circumstances. If not qualified to do this for themselves, they should seek professional advice. The decision to invest or trade is for the individual alone. The author expressly disclaims all and any liability to any person, with respect of anything, and of the consequences of anything, done or omitted to be done by any such person in reliance upon the whole or any part of the contents in this book.

Investing and trading involve risk of loss. Past results are not necessarily indicative of future results.

Peter Castle is not a licensed investment adviser.

www.ingramcontent.com/pod-product-compliance
Ingram Content Group UK Ltd.
Pitfield, Milton Keynes, MK11 3LW, UK
UKHW050632110425
457266UK00005B/12